# Student Solutions Manual

## for

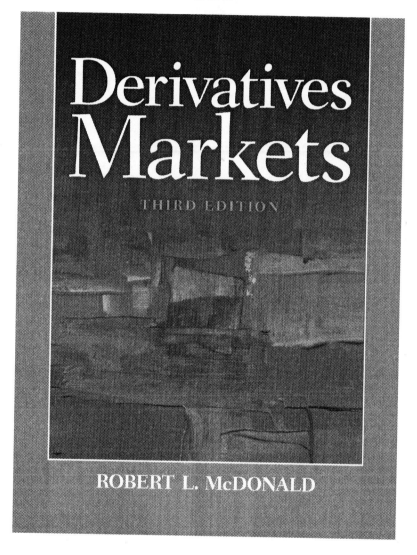

Derivatives Markets

THIRD EDITION

ROBERT L. McDONALD

# Rüdiger Fahlenbrach

École Polytechnique Fédérale de Lausanne

**PEARSON**

Boston  Columbus  Indianapolis  New York  San Francisco  Upper Saddle River
Amsterdam  Cape Town  Dubai  London  Madrid  Milan  Munich  Paris  Montreal  Toronto
Delhi  Mexico City  Sao Paulo  Sydney  Hong Kong  Seoul  Singapore  Taipei  Tokyo

Acquisitions Editor: Katie Rowland
Editorial Product Manager, Jill Kolongowski
Senior Production Project Manager: Kathryn Dinovo
Senior Manufacturing Buyer: Carol Melville

10 9 8 7 6 5 4 3 2

www.pearsonhighered.com

**PEARSON**

ISBN-10:    0-13-611828-3
ISBN-13: 978-0-13-611828-2

# Contents

©2013 Pearson Education, Inc. Publishing as Prentice Hall

iv Contents

# Chapter 1

## Introduction to Derivatives

### Question 1.2

A variety of counterparties are imaginable. For one, we could think about speculators who have differences in opinion and who do not believe that we will have excessive temperature variations during the life of the futures contracts. Thus, they are willing to take the opposing side, receiving a payoff if the weather is stable.

Alternatively, there may be opposing hedging needs: Compare the ski-resort operator and the soft drink manufacturer. The cooling-degree-day futures contract will pay off if the weather is relatively mild, and we saw that the resort operator will buy the futures contract. The buyer of the cooling-degree-day futures will make a loss if the weather is cold (which means that the seller of the contract will make a gain). Since the soft drink manufacturer wants additional money if it is cold, she may be interested in taking the opposite side of the cooling-degree-day futures.

### Question 1.4

In this problem, the brokerage fee is variable and depends on the actual dollar amount of the sale/purchase of the shares. The concept of the transaction cost remains the same: If you buy the shares, the commission is added to the amount you owe, and if you sell the shares, the commission is deducted from the proceeds of the sale.

a)
$$(\$41.05 \times 100) + (\$41.05 \times 100) \times 0.003 = \$4{,}117.315$$
$$= \$4{,}117.32$$

b)
$$(\$40.95 \times 100) - (\$40.95 \times 100) \times 0.003 = \$4{,}082.715$$
$$= \$4{,}082.72$$

c)
$$\$4{,}117.32 - \$4{,}082.72 = \$34.6$$

The variable (or proportional) brokerage fee is advantageous to us. Our round-trip transaction fees are reduced by $15.40.

### Question 1.6

A short sale of XYZ entails borrowing shares of XYZ and then selling them and receiving cash. Therefore, initially, we will receive the proceeds from the sale of the asset less the proportional commission charge:

$$300 \times (\$30.19) - 300 \times (\$30.19) \times 0.005 = \$9{,}057 \times 0.995$$
$$= \$9{,}011.72$$

When we close out the position, we will again incur the commission charge, which is added to the purchasing cost:

$$300 \times (\$29.87) + 300 \times (\$29.87) \times 0.005 = \$8,961 \times 1.005$$
$$= \$9,005.81$$

Finally, we subtract the cost of covering the short position from our initial proceeds to receive total profits: $\$9,011.72 - \$9,005.81 = \$5.91$. We can see that paying the commission charge twice significantly reduces the profits we can make.

## Question 1.8

We learned from the main text that short selling is equivalent to borrowing money and that a short seller will often have to deposit the proceeds of the short sale with the lender as collateral.

A short seller is entitled to earn interest on his collateral, and the interest rate he earns is called the short rebate in the stock market. Usually, the short rebate is close to the prevailing market interest rate. Sometimes, though, a particular stock is scarce and difficult to borrow. In this case, the short rebate is substantially less than the current market interest rate, and an equity lender can earn a nice profit in the form of the difference between the current market interest rate and the short rebate.

By signing an agreement as mentioned in the problem, you give your brokerage firm the possibility to act as an equity lender, using the shares of your account. Brokers want you to sign such an agreement because they can make additional profits.

## Question 1.10

The main textbook explains short selling as follows. "The sale of a stock you do not already own is called a short-sale." Short positions are those resulting from short sales. At NASDAQ for example, each financial firm is required to report its overall short positions in all accounts in NASDAQ-listed securities twice a month. The short positions from these reports are aggregated and the resulting number is called short interest in NASDAQ stocks. The short interest statistics are widely observed, and some financial market participants believe that short interest is a good measure of market sentiment.

You can easily access statistics on short interest on individual stocks on Nasdaq (www.nasdaq.com). Once you are on the home page, go to the pull-down menu "Quotes and Research," then go to "Short Interest" in the folder "Company Profile." Once you are on that page, you can enter up to 25 tickers and retrieve the short interest in the stocks of your choice.

In general, stocks that lend themselves to some speculation and stocks around corporate events (mergers and acquisition, dividend dates, etc.) with uncertain outcomes will have a particularly high short interest.

It is theoretically possible to have short interest of more than 100 percent because some market participants (e.g., market makers) have the ability to short sell a stock without having a locate (i.e., having someone who actually owns the stock and has agreed to lend it).

## Question 1.12

We are interested in borrowing the asset "money" to buy a house. Therefore, we go to an owner of the asset, called Bank. The Bank provides the dollar amount, say $250,000, in digital form in our mortgage account. As $250,000 is a large amount of money, the bank is subject to substantial **credit risk** (e.g., we may lose our job) and demands a **collateral.** Although the money itself is not subject to large variations in price (besides inflation risk, it is difficult to imagine a reason for money to vary in value), the Bank knows that we want to buy a house, and real estate prices vary substantially. Therefore, the Bank wants more collateral than the $250,000 they are lending.

In fact, as the Bank is only lending up to 80 percent of the value of the house, we could get a mortgage of $250,000 for a house that is worth $250,000 ÷ 0.8 = $312,500. We see that the bank factored in a **haircut** of $312,500 − $250,000 = $62,500 to protect itself from credit risk and adverse fluctuations in property prices.

We buy back the asset money over a long horizon of time by reducing our mortgage through annuity payments.

## Question 1.14

We have the following for the different trades and different dealers:

a)

|         | A    | B   | C    |
|---------|------|-----|------|
| Trade 1 | +5   | −5  |      |
| Trade 2 | +15  |     | −15  |
| Trade 3 |      | +10 | −10  |
| Trade 4 | −20  |     | +20  |
| Total   | 0    | +5  | −5   |

Therefore, trader A's net position is zero, trader B is long five contracts, and trader C is short five contracts.

b)  Trading volume is equal to 5 + 15 + 10 + 20 = 50.

Open interest is equal to 5.

Notional value of trading volume is equal to 50 contracts × $100/contract = $5,000

Notional value of open interest is equal to 5 contracts × $ 100/contract = $500.

c) Now all traders have a net position of zero. Trading volume has increased by five contracts to 55. The notional value of trading volume is equal to $55 \times \$100 = \$5,500$. Open interest and the notional value of open interest are equal to zero.

d) Trading volume and open interest would be identical; the notional values of trading volume and open interest would be lower.

# Chapter 2

## An Introduction to Forwards and Options

### Question 2.2

Since we sold the stock initially, our payoff at expiration from being short the stock is negative.

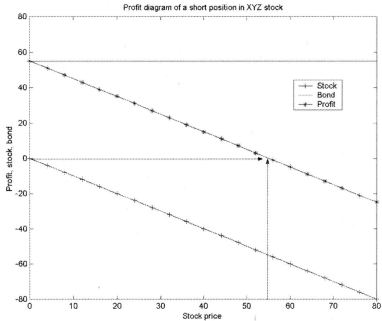

In order to obtain the profit diagram at expiration, we have to lend out the money we received from the short sale of the stock. We do so by buying a bond for $50. After one year, we receive from the investment in the bond: $50 \times (1 + 0.1) = $55. The second figure shows the graph of the sold stock, of the money we receive from the investment in the bond, and of the sum of the two positions, which is the profit graph. The arrows show that at a stock price of $55, the profit at expiration is indeed zero.

## Question 2.4

a) The payoff to a long forward at expiration is equal to:

Payoff to long forward = Spot price at expiration – forward price

Therefore, we can construct the following table:

| Price of asset in six months | Agreed forward price | Payoff to the long forward |
|:---:|:---:|:---:|
| 40 | 50 | −10 |
| 45 | 50 | −5 |
| 50 | 50 | 0 |
| 55 | 50 | 5 |
| 60 | 50 | 10 |

b) The payoff to a purchased call option at expiration is:

Payoff to call option = max[0, spot price at expiration – strike price]

The strike is given: It is $50. Therefore, we can construct the following table:

| Price of asset in six months | Strike price | Payoff to the call option |
|:---:|:---:|:---:|
| 40 | 50 | 0 |
| 45 | 50 | 0 |
| 50 | 50 | 0 |
| 55 | 50 | 5 |
| 60 | 50 | 10 |

c) If we compare the two contracts, we immediately see that the call option has a protection for adverse movements in the price of the asset: If the spot price is below $50, the buyer of the call option can walk away and need not incur a loss. The buyer of the long forward incurs a loss, but he has the same payoff as the buyer of the call option if the spot price is above $50. Therefore, the call option should be more expensive. It is this attractive option to walk away that we have to pay for.

## Question 2.6

We need to solve the following equation to determine the effective annual interest rate: $\$91 \times (1 + r)$ = $\$100$. We obtain $r = 0.0989$, which means that the effective annual interest rate is approximately 9.9 percent.

Remember that when we drew profit diagrams for the forward or call option, we drew the payoff on the vertical axis, and the index price at the expiration of the contract on the horizontal axis. In this case, the particularity is that the default-free, zero-coupon bond will pay exactly $\$100$, no matter what the stock price is. Therefore, the payoff diagram is just a horizontal line, intersecting the $y$-axis at $\$100$.

The textbook provides the answer to the question concerning the profit diagram in the section "Zero-Coupon Bonds in Payoff and Profit Diagrams." When we were calculating profits, we saw that we had to find the future value of the initial investment. In this case, our initial investment is $\$91$. How do we find the future value? We use the current risk-free interest rate and multiply the initial investment by it. However, as our bond is default-free and does not bear coupons, the effective annual interest rate is exactly the 9.9 percent we have calculated before. Therefore, the future value of $\$91$ is $\$91 \times (1 + 0.0989) = \$100$, and our profit in six months is zero!

## Question 2.8

We saw in question 2.7 (b) that there is no advantage in buying either the stock or the forward contract if we can borrow to buy a stock today (so both strategies do not require any initial cash) and if the profit from this strategy is the same as the profit of a long forward contract. The profit of a long forward contract with a price for delivery of $\$53$ is equal to: $\$S_T - \$53$, where $S_T$ is the (unknown) value of one share of XYZ at expiration of the forward contract in one year. If we borrow $\$50$ today to buy one share of XYZ stock (that costs $\$50$), we have to repay in one year: $\$50 \times (1 + r)$. Our total profit in one year from borrowing to buy one share of XYZ is therefore: $\$S_T - \$50 \times (1 + r)$. Now we can equate the two profit equations and solve for the interest rate $r$:

$$\$S_T - \$53 = \$S_T - \$50 \times (1 + r)$$
$$\Leftrightarrow \$53 = \$50 \times (1 + r)$$
$$\Leftrightarrow \frac{\$53}{\$50} - 1 = r$$
$$\Leftrightarrow r = 0.06$$

Therefore, the one-year effective interest rate that is consistent with no advantage to either buying the stock or forward contract is 6 percent.

## Question 2.10

a) Figure 2.6 depicts the profit from a long call option on the S&R index with six months to expiration and a strike price of $1,000 if the future price of the option premium is $95.68. The profit of the long call option is:

$$\max[0, S_T - \$1,000] - \$95.68$$

$$\Leftrightarrow \max[-\$95.68, S_T - \$1,095.68]$$

where $S_T$ is the (unknown) value of the S&R index at expiration of the call option in six months. In order to find the S&R index price at which the call option diagram intersects the $x$-axis, we have to set the above equation equal to zero. We get: $S_T - \$1,095.68 = 0 \Leftrightarrow S_T = \$1,095.68$. This is the only solution, as the other part of the maximum function, $-\$95.68$, is always less than zero.

b) The profit of the six month forward contract with a forward price of $1,020 is: $\$S_T - \$1,020$. In order to find the S&R index price at which the call option and the forward contract have the same profit, we need to set both parts of the maximum function of the profit of the call option equal to the profit of the forward contract and see which part permits a solution. First, we see immediately that $\$S_T - \$1,020 = \$S_T - \$1,095.68$ does not have a solution. But we can solve the other leg: $\$S_T - \$1,020 = -\$95.68 \Leftrightarrow S_T = \$924.32$, which is the value given in the exercise.

## Question 2.12

a) Long Forward

The maximum loss occurs if the stock price at expiration is zero (the stock price cannot be less than zero because companies have limited liability). The forward then pays 0 – Forward price. The maximum gain is unlimited. The stock price at expiration could theoretically grow to infinity; there is no bound. We make a lot of money if the stock price grows to infinity (or to a very large amount).

b) Short Forward

The profit for a short forward contract is forward price – stock price at expiration. The maximum loss occurs if the stock price rises sharply; there is no bound to it, so it could grow to infinity. The maximum gain occurs if the stock price is zero.

c) Long Call

We will not exercise the call option if the stock price at expiration is less than the strike price. Consequently, the only thing we lose is the future value of the premium we paid initially to buy the option. As the stock price can grow very large (and without bound), and our payoff grows linearly in the terminal stock price once it is higher than the strike, there is no limit to our gain.

d) Short Call

We have no control over the exercise decision when we write a call. The buyer of the call option decides whether to exercise it or not, and he will only exercise the call if he makes a profit. As we have the opposite side, we will never make any money at the expiration of the call option. Our profit is restricted to the future value of the premium, and we make this maximum profit whenever the stock price at expiration is smaller than the strike price. However, the stock price at expiration can be very large and has no bound, and as our loss grows linearly in the terminal stock price, there is no limit to our loss.

e) Long Put

We will not exercise the put option if the stock price at expiration is larger than the strike price. Consequently, the only thing we lose whenever the terminal stock price is larger than the strike is the future value of the premium we paid initially to buy the option. We will profit from a decline in the stock prices. However, stock prices cannot be smaller than zero, so our maximum gain is restricted to strike price less the future value of the premium, and it occurs at a terminal stock price of zero.

f) Short Put

We have no control over the exercise decision when we write a put. The buyer of the put option decides whether to exercise or not, and he will only exercise if he makes a profit. As we have the opposite side, we will never make any money at the expiration of the put option. Our profit is restricted to the future value of the premium, and we make this maximum profit whenever the stock price at expiration is greater than the strike price. However, we lose money whenever the stock price is smaller than the strike; hence, the largest loss occurs when the stock price attains its smallest possible value, zero. We lose the strike price because somebody sells us an asset for the strike that is worth nothing. We are only compensated by the future value of the premium we received.

## Question 2.14

In order to be able to draw profit diagrams, we need to find the future values of the put premia. They are:

a) 35-strike put: $1.53 \times (1 + 0.08) = \$1.6524$

b) 40-strike put: $3.26 \times (1 + 0.08) = \$3.5208$

c) 45-strike put: $5.75 \times (1 + 0.08) = \$6.21$

We get the following payoff diagrams:

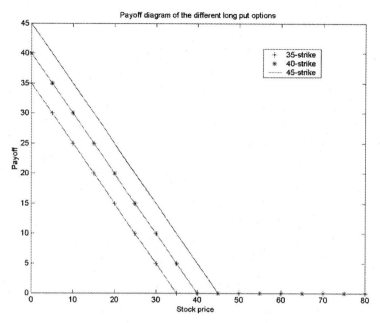

We get the profit diagram by deducting the option premia from the payoff graphs. The profit diagram looks as follows:

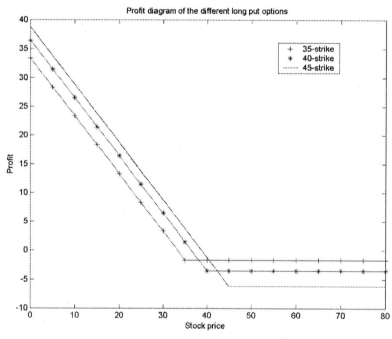

Intuitively, whenever the 35-strike put option pays off (i.e., has a payoff bigger than zero), the 40-strike and the 35-strike options also pay off. However, there are some instances in which the 40-strike option pays off and the 35-strike option does not. Similarly, there are some instances in which the 45-strike option pays off but neither the 40-strike nor the 35-strike pay off. Therefore, the 45-strike offers more potential than the 40- and 35-strike, and the 40-strike offers more potential than the 35-strike. We pay for these additional payoff possibilities by initially paying a higher premium. It makes sense that the premium is increasing in the strike price.

## Question 2.16

The following is a copy of a spreadsheet that solves the problem:

| | A | B | C | D | E | F | G | H | I |
|---|---|---|---|---|---|---|---|---|---|
| 1 | | | | Options | | | Forward | | |
| 2 | | | | | | | | | |
| 3 | stock price at | 50 | | strike price: | 45 | | forward price | 45 | |
| 4 | interest rate | 0.08 | | call premium: | 8.21 | | | | |
| 5 | | | | put premium | 5.22 | | | | |
| 6 | | | | | | | | | |
| 7 | Long positions: | | | | | | | | |
| 8 | | | | | | | | | |
| 9 | payoff call opt | =MAX(0,B3-E3) | | | | | | | |
| 10 | profit call optic | =MAX(0,B3-E3)-(1+B4)*E4 | | | | | | | |
| 11 | payoff put opt | =MAX(0,E3-B3) | | | | | | | |
| 12 | profit put optic | =MAX(0,E3-B3)-(1+B4)*E5 | | | | | | | |
| 13 | payoff/profit f | =B3-H3 | | | | | | | |
| 14 | | | | | | | | | |
| 15 | Short positions: | | | | | | | | |
| 16 | | | | | | | | | |
| 17 | payoff call opt | =-MAX(0,B3-E3) | | | | | | | |
| 18 | profit call optic | =-(MAX(0,B3-E3)-(1+B4)*E4) | | | | | | | |
| 19 | payoff put opt | =-MAX(0,E3-B3) | | | | | | | |
| 20 | profit put optic | =-(MAX(0,E3-B3)-(1+B4)*E5) | | | | | | | |
| 21 | payoff/profit f | =H3-B3 | | | | | | | |
| 22 | | | | | | | | | |
| 23 | | | | | | | | | |

# Chapter 3

## Insurance, Collars, and Other Strategies

### Question 3.2

This question constructs a position that is the opposite to the position of Table 3.1. Therefore, we should get the exact opposite results from Table 3.1. and the associated figures. Mimicking Table 3.1., we indeed have:

| S&R Index | S&R Put | Payoff | −(Cost + Interest) | Profit |
|---|---|---|---|---|
| −900.00 | −100.00 | −1,000.00 | 1,095.68 | 95.68 |
| −950.00 | −50.00 | −1,000.00 | 1,095.68 | 95.68 |
| −1,000.00 | 0.00 | −1,000.00 | 1,095.68 | 95.68 |
| −1,050.00 | 0.00 | −1,050.00 | 1,095.68 | 45.68 |
| −1,100.00 | 0.00 | −1,100.00 | 1,095.68 | −4.32 |
| −1,150.00 | 0.00 | −1,150.00 | 1,095.68 | −54.32 |
| −1,200.00 | 0.00 | −1,200.00 | 1,095.68 | −104.32 |

On the next page, we see the corresponding payoff and profit diagrams. Please note that they match the combined payoff and profit diagrams of Figure 3.5. Only the axes have different scales.

Payoff diagram:

Profit diagram:

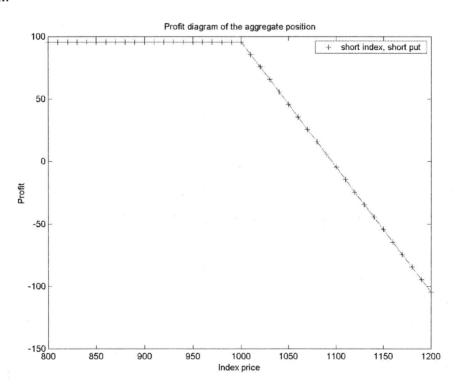

## Question 3.4

This question is another application of Put-Call-Parity. Initially, we have the following cost to enter into the combined position: We receive $1,000 from the short sale of the index, and we have to pay the call premium. Therefore, the future value of our cost is: ($120.405 − $1,000) × (1 + 0.02) = −$897.19. Note that a negative cost means that we initially have an inflow of money.

Now, we can directly proceed to draw the payoff diagram:

We can clearly see from the figure that the payoff graph of the short index and the long call looks like a fixed obligation of $950, which is alleviated by a long put position with a strike price of 950. The following profit diagram, including the cost for the combined position, confirms this:

## Question 3.6

We now move from a graphical representation and verification of the Put-Call-Parity to a mathematical representation. Let us first consider the payoff of (a). If we buy the index (let us name it S), we receive at the time of expiration T of the options simply $S_T$.

The payoffs of part (b) are a little bit more complicated. If we deal with options and the maximum function, it is convenient to split the future values of the index into two regions: one where $S_T < K$ and another one where $S_T \geq K$. We then look at each region separately, and hope to be able to draw a conclusion when we look at the aggregate position.

We have for the payoffs in (b):

| Instrument | $S_T < K = 950$ | $S_T \geq K = 950$ |
|---|---|---|
| Get repayment of loan | $931.37 \times 1.02 = \$950$ | $931.37 \times 1.02 = \$950$ |
| Long call option | max $(S_T - 950, 0) = 0$ | $S_T - 950$ |
| Short put option | $- \max (\$950 - S_T, 0)$ | $0$ |
| | $= S_T - \$950$ | |
| Total | $S_T$ | $S_T$ |

We now see that the total aggregate position only gives us $S_T$, no matter what the final index value is—but this is the same payoff as in part (a). Our proof for the payoff equivalence is complete.

Now let us turn to the profits. If we buy the index today, we need to finance it. Therefore, we borrow $1,000 and have to repay $1,020 after one year. The profit for part (a) is thus: $S_T - \$1,020$.

The profits of the aggregate position in part (b) are the payoffs, less the future value of the call premium plus the future value of the put premium (because we have sold the put), and less the future value of the loan we gave initially. Note that we already know that a riskless bond is canceling out of the profit calculations. We can again tabulate:

| Instrument | $S_T < K$ | $S_T \geq K$ |
|---|---|---|
| Get repayment of loan | $931.37 \times 1.02 = \$950$ | $931.37 \times 1.02 = \$950$ |
| Future value of given loan | $-\$950$ | $-\$950$ |
| Long call option | max $(S_T - 950, 0) = 0$ | $S_T - 950$ |
| Future value call premium | $-\$120.405 \times 1.02 = -\$122.81$ | $-\$120.405 \times 1.02 = -\$122.81$ |
| Short put option | $- \max (\$950 - S_T, 0)$ | $0$ |
| | $= S_T - \$950$ | |
| Future value put premium | $\$51.777 \times 1.02 = \$52.81$ | $\$51.777 \times 1.02 = \$52.81$ |
| Total | $S_T - 1020$ | $S_T - 1020$ |

Indeed, we see that the profits for parts (a) and (b) are identical as well.

## Question 3.8

This question is a direct application of the Put-Call-Parity. We will use equation (3.1) in the following and input the given variables:

$$Call\,(K,\,t\,) - Put\,(K,\,t\,) = PV\,(F_{0,t} - K\,)$$

$$\Leftrightarrow Call\,(K,\,t\,) - Put\,(K,\,t\,) - PV\,(F_{0,t}\,) = -PV\,(K\,)$$

$$\Leftrightarrow Call\,(K,\,t\,) - Put\,(K,\,t\,) - S_0 = -PV\,(K\,)$$

$$\Leftrightarrow \$109.20 - \$60.18 - \$1{,}000 = -\frac{K}{1.02}$$

$$\Leftrightarrow K = \$970.00$$

## Question 3.10

The strategy of selling a call (or put) and buying a call (or put) at a higher strike is called call (put) bear spread. In order to draw the profit diagrams, we need to find the future value of the cost of entering in the bull spread positions. We have:

Cost of call bear spread: $(\$71.802 - \$120.405) \times 1.02 = -\$49.575$
Cost of put bear spread: $(\$101.214 - \$51.777) \times 1.02 = \$50.426$

The payoff diagram shows that the payoff to the call bear spread is uniformly less than the payoffs to the put bear spread. The difference is exactly $100, equal to the difference in strikes and as well equal to the difference in the future value of the costs of the spreads.

There is a difference, because the call bear spread has a negative initial cost (i.e., we are receiving money if we enter into it).

The higher initial cost for the put bear spread is exactly offset by the higher payoff so that the profits of both strategies turn out to be the same. It is easy to show this with equation (3.1), the put-call-parity.

Payoff diagram:

Profit diagram:

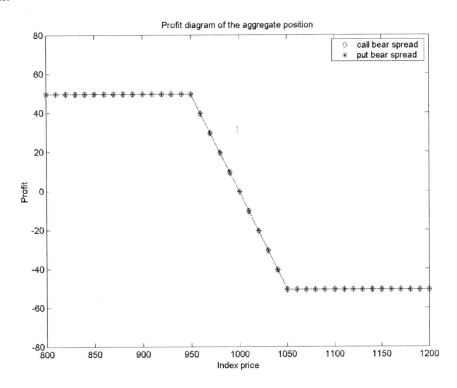

## Question 3.12

Our initial cash required to put on the collar, i.e. the net option premium, is as follows: −$51.873 + $51.777 = −$0.096. Therefore, we receive only 10 cents if we enter into this collar. The position is very close to a zero-cost collar.

The profit diagram looks as follows:

If we compare this profit diagram with the profit diagram of the previous exercise (3.11.), we see that we traded in the additional call premium (that limited our losses after index decreases) against more participation on the upside. Please note that both maximum loss and gain are higher than in question 3.11.

## Question 3.14

a)  This question deals with the option trading strategy known as Box spread. We saw earlier that if we deal with options and the maximum function, it is convenient to split the future values of the index into different regions. Let us name the final value of the S&R index $S_T$. We have two strike prices; therefore, we will use three regions: one in which $S_T < 950$, one in which $950 \leq S_T < 1,000$, and another one in which $S_T \geq 1,000$. We then look at each region separately and hope to be able to see that indeed when we aggregate, there is no S&R risk when we look at the aggregate position.

| Instrument | $S_T < 950$ | $950 \le S_T < 1{,}000$ | $S_T \ge 1{,}000$ |
|---|---|---|---|
| Long 950 call | 0 | $S_T - \$950$ | $S_T - \$950$ |
| Short 1,000 call | 0 | 0 | $\$1{,}000 - S_T$ |
| Short 950 put | $S_T - \$950$ | 0 | 0 |
| Long 1,000 put | $\$1{,}000 - S_T$ | $\$1{,}000 - S_T$ | 0 |
| Total | $50 | $50 | $50 |

We see that there is no occurrence of the final index value in the row labeled total. The option position does not contain S&R price risk.

b) The initial cost is the sum of the long option premia less the premia we receive for the sold options. We have:

$$\text{Cost } \$120.405 - \$93.809 - \$51.77 + \$74.201 = \$49.027$$

c) The payoff of the position after six months is $50, as we can see from the above table.

d) The implicit interest rate of the cash flows is: $\$50.00 \div \$49.027 = 1.019 \sim= 1.02$. The implicit interest rate is indeed 2 percent.

## Question 3.16

A bull spread or a bear spread can never have an initial premium of zero because we are buying the same number of calls (or puts) that we are selling and the two legs of the bull and bear spreads have different strikes. A zero initial premium would mean that two calls (or puts) with different strikes have the same price—and we know by now that two instruments that have different payoff structures and the same underlying risk cannot have the same price without creating an arbitrage opportunity.

A symmetric butterfly spread cannot have a premium of zero because it would violate the convexity condition of options.

## Question 3.18

The following three figures show the individual legs of each of the three suggested strategies. The last subplot shows the aggregate position. It is evident from the figures that you can indeed use all the suggested strategies to construct the same butterfly spread. Another method to show the claim of 3.18. mathematically would be to establish the equivalence by using the Put-Call-Parity on (b) and (c) and show that you can write it in terms of the instruments of (a).

## Profit diagram part (a)

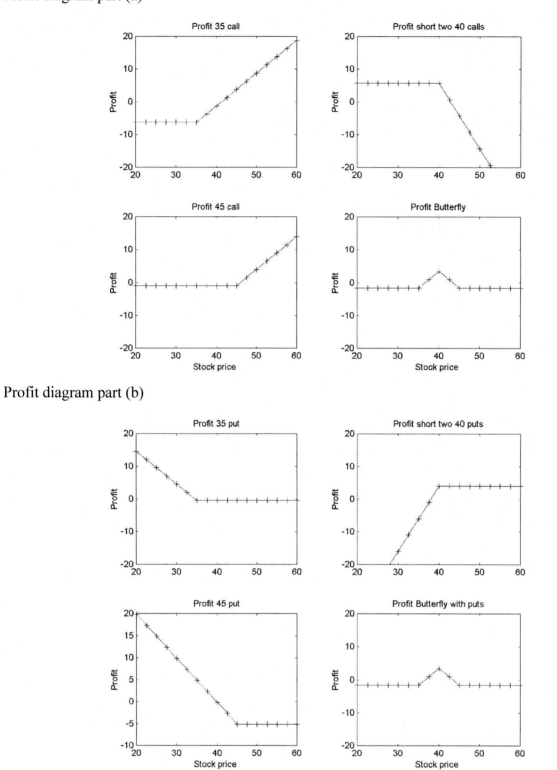

## Profit diagram part (b)

Profit diagram part (c)

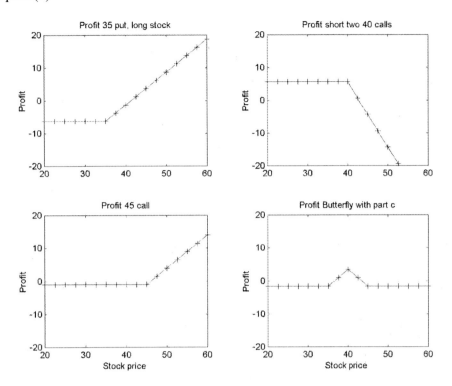

## Question 3.20

Use separate cells for the strike price and the quantities you buy and sell for each strike (i.e., make use of the plus or minus sign). Then, use the maximum function to calculate payoffs and profits.

The best way to solve this problem is probably to have the calculations necessary for the payoff and profit diagrams run in the background (e.g., in another auxiliary table that you are referencing). Define the boundaries for the calculations dynamically and symmetrically around the current stock price. Then use the diagram function with the line style to draw the diagrams.

# Chapter 4

## Introduction to Risk Management

### Question 4.2

If the forward price were $0.80 instead of $1, we would get the following table:

| Copper price in one year | Total cost | Unhedged profit | Profit on short forward | Net income on hedged profit |
|---|---|---|---|---|
| $0.70 | — $0.90 = | −$0.20 | .80−.70 = $0.10 | −$0.10 |
| $0.80 | $0.90 | −$0.10 | .80−.80 $0 | −$0.10 |
| $0.90 | $0.90 | 0 | .80−.90 −$0.10 | −$0.10 |
| $1.00 | $0.90 | $0.10 | .80−1.00 −$0.20 | −$0.10 |
| $1.10 | $0.90 | $0.20 | −$0.30 | −$0.10 |
| $1.20 | $0.90 | $0.30 | −$0.40 | −$0.10 |

With a forward price of $0.45, we have:

| Copper price in one year | Total cost | Unhedged profit | Profit on short forward | Net income on hedged profit |
|---|---|---|---|---|
| $0.70 | $0.90 | −$0.20 | −$0.25 | −$0.45 |
| $0.80 | $0.90 | −$0.10 | −$0.35 | −$0.45 |
| $0.90 | $0.90 | 0 | −$0.45 | −$0.45 |
| $1.00 | $0.90 | $0.10 | −$0.55 | −$0.45 |
| $1.10 | $0.90 | $0.20 | −$0.65 | −$0.45 |
| $1.20 | $0.90 | $0.30 | −$0.75 | −$0.45 |

Although the copper forward price of $0.45 is below our total costs of $0.90, it is higher than the variable cost of $0.40. It still makes sense to produce copper because even at a price of $0.45 in one year, we will be able to partially cover our fixed costs.

## Question 4.4

We will explicitly calculate the profit for the $1.00-strike and show figures for all three strikes. The future value of the $1.00-strike call premium amounts to: $0.0376 \times 1.062 = $0.04$.

| Copper price in one year | Total cost | Unhedged profit | Profit on short $1.00-strike call option | Call premium received | Net income on hedged profit |
|---|---|---|---|---|---|
| $0.70 | $0.90 | −$0.20 | 0 | $0.04 | −$0.16 |
| $0.80 | $0.90 | −$0.10 | 0 | $0.04 | −$0.06 |
| $0.90 | $0.90 | 0 | 0 | $0.04 | $0.04 |
| $1.00 | $0.90 | $0.10 | 0 | $0.04 | $0.14 |
| $1.10 | $0.90 | $0.20 | −$0.10 | $0.04 | $0.14 |
| $1.20 | $0.90 | $0.30 | −$0.20 | $0.04 | $0.14 |

We obtain the following payoff graphs:

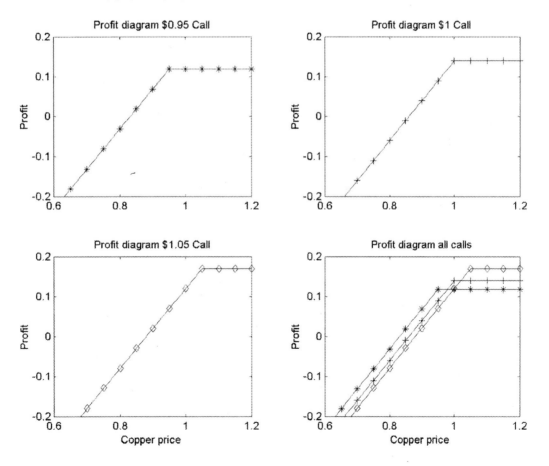

# Question 4.6

a)

| Copper price in one year | Total cost | Profit on short $1.025 put | Profit on two long $0.975 puts | Net premium | Hedged profit |
|---|---|---|---|---|---|
| $0.70 | $0.90 | −$0.325 | $0.55 | $0.0022 | $0.0228 |
| $0.80 | $0.90 | −$0.225 | $0.35 | $0.0022 | $0.0228 |
| $0.90 | $0.90 | −$0.125 | $0.150 | $0.0022 | $0.0228 |
| $1.00 | $0.90 | −$0.025 | 0 | $0.0022 | $0.0728 |
| $1.10 | $0.90 | 0 | 0 | $0.0022 | $0.1978 |
| $1.20 | $0.90 | 0 | 0 | $0.0022 | $0.2978 |

We can see from the profit diagram on the following page (and the above table) that in the case of a favorable increase in copper prices, the hedged profit is almost identical to the unhedged profit.

Profit diagram:

b)

| Copper price in one year | Total cost | Profit on two short $1.034 put | Profit on three long $1 puts | Net premium | Hedged profit |
|---|---|---|---|---|---|
| $0.70 | $0.90 | −$0.6680 | $0.9 | $0.0002 | $0.0318 |
| $0.80 | $0.90 | −$0.4680 | $0.6 | $0.0002 | $0.0318 |
| $0.90 | $0.90 | −$0.2680 | $0.3 | $0.0002 | $0.0318 |
| $1.00 | $0.90 | −$0.0680 | 0 | $0.0002 | $0.0318 |
| $1.10 | $0.90 | 0 | 0 | $0.0002 | $0.1998 |
| $1.20 | $0.90 | 0 | 0 | $0.0002 | $0.2998 |

We can see from the profit diagram on the following page (and the above table) that in the case of a favorable increase in copper prices, the hedged profit is almost identical to the unhedged profit.

Profit diagram:

# Question 4.8

In this exercise, we need to first find the future value of the call premia. For the $1-strike call, it is: $0.0376 × 1.062 = $0.04. The following table shows the profit calculations of the $1.00-strike call. The calculations for the two other calls are exactly similar. The figures on the next page compare the profit diagrams of all three possible hedging strategies.

| Copper price in one year | Total cost | Unhedged profit | Profit on long $1.00-strike call | Call premium | Net income on hedged profit |
|---|---|---|---|---|---|
| $0.70 | $5.70 | $0.50 | 0 | $0.04 | $0.46 |
| $0.80 | $5.80 | $0.40 | 0 | $0.04 | $0.36 |
| $0.90 | $5.90 | $0.30 | 0 | $0.04 | $0.26 |
| $1.00 | $6.00 | $0.20 | 0 | $0.04 | $0.16 |
| $1.10 | $6.10 | $0.10 | $0.10 | $0.04 | $0.16 |
| $1.20 | $6.20 | 0 | $0.20 | $0.04 | $0.16 |

We obtain the following profit diagrams:

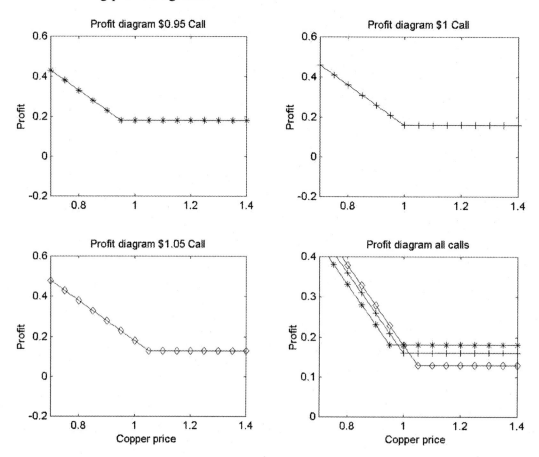

## Question 4.10

Telco will sell collars, which means that they buy the call leg and sell the put leg. We have to compute for each case the net option premium position, and find its future value. We have for:

a)  ($0.0376 − $0.0178) × 1.062 = $0.021

b)  ($0.0274 − $0.0265) × 1.062 = $0.001

c)  ($0.0649 − $0.0178) × 1.062 = $0.050

a)

| Copper price in one year | Total cost | Unhedged profit | Profit on short $0.95 put | Profit on long $1.00 call | Net premium | Hedged profit |
|---|---|---|---|---|---|---|
| $0.70 | $5.70 | $0.50 | −$0.25 | 0 | $0.021 | $0.2290 |
| $0.80 | $5.80 | $0.40 | −$0.15 | 0 | $0.021 | $0.2290 |
| $0.90 | $5.90 | $0.30 | −$0.05 | 0 | $0.021 | $0.2290 |
| $1.00 | $6.00 | $0.20 | $0 | 0 | $0.021 | $0.1790 |
| $1.10 | $6.10 | $0.10 | 0 | $0.10 | $0.021 | $0.1790 |
| $1.20 | $6.20 | 0 | 0 | $0.20 | $0.021 | $0.1790 |

Profit diagram:

b)

| Copper price in one year | Total cost | Unhedged profit | Profit on short $0.975 put | Profit on long $1.025 call | Net premium | Hedged profit |
|---|---|---|---|---|---|---|
| $0.70 | $5.70 | $0.50 | −$0.275 | 0 | $0.001 | $0.2240 |
| $0.80 | $5.80 | $0.40 | −$0.175 | 0 | $0.001 | $0.2240 |
| $0.90 | $5.90 | $0.30 | −$0.075 | 0 | $0.001 | $0.2240 |
| $1.00 | $6.00 | $0.20 | $0 | 0 | $0.001 | $0.1990 |
| $1.10 | $6.10 | $0.10 | 0 | $0.0750 | $0.001 | $0.1740 |
| $1.20 | $6.20 | 0 | 0 | $0.1750 | $0.001 | $0.1740 |

Profit diagram:

c)

| Copper price in one year | Total cost | Unhedged profit | Profit on short $0.95 put | Profit on long $0.95 call | Net premium | Hedged profit |
|---|---|---|---|---|---|---|
| $0.70 | $5.70 | $0.50 | −$0.25 | 0 | $0.05 | $0.2 |
| $0.80 | $5.80 | $0.40 | −$0.15 | 0 | $0.05 | $0.2 |
| $0.90 | $5.90 | $0.30 | −$0.05 | 0 | $0.05 | $0.2 |
| $1.00 | $6.00 | $0.20 | 0 | $0.050 | $0.05 | $0.2 |
| $1.10 | $6.10 | $0.10 | 0 | $0.150 | $0.05 | $0.2 |
| $1.20 | $6.20 | 0 | 0 | $0.250 | $0.05 | $0.2 |

We see that we are completely and perfectly hedged. Buying a collar where the put and call leg have equal strike prices perfectly offsets the copper price risk.

Profit diagram:

## Question 4.12

This is a very important exercise to really understand the benefits and pitfalls of hedging strategies. Wirco needs copper as an input, which means that its costs increase with the price of copper. We may, therefore, think that they need to hedge against increases in the copper price. However, we must not forget that the price of wire, the source of Wirco's revenues, also depends positively on the price of copper: The price Wirco can obtain for one unit of wire is $50 plus the price of copper. We will see that those copper price risks cancel each other out. Mathematically,

$$\text{Wirco's cost per unit of wire:} \quad \$3 + \$1.50 + S_T$$

$$\text{Wirco's revenue per unit of wire: } \$5 + S_T$$

and $S_T$ is the price of copper after one year. Therefore, we can determine Wirco's profits as:

$$\text{Profit} = \text{Revenue} - \text{Cost} = \$5 + S_T - (\$3 + \$1.50 + S_T) = \$0.50$$

We see that the profits of Wirco do not depend on the price of copper. Cost and revenue copper price risk cancel each other out. In this situation, if we buy a long forward contract, we do in fact introduce copper price risk! To understand this, add a long forward contract to the profit equation:

$$\text{Profit with forward:} = \$5 + S_T - (\$3 + \$1.50 + S_T) + S_T - \$1 = S_T - \$0.50$$

To summarize,

| Copper price in one year | Total cost | Total revenue | Unhedged profit | Profit on long forward | Net income on 'hedged' profit |
|---|---|---|---|---|---|
| $0.70 | $5.20 | $5.70 | $0.50 | −$0.30 | $0.20 |
| $0.80 | $5.30 | $5.80 | $0.50 | −$0.20 | $0.30 |
| $0.90 | $5.40 | $5.90 | $0.50 | −$0.10 | $0.40 |
| $1.00 | $5.50 | $6.00 | $0.50 | 0 | $0.50 |
| $1.10 | $5.60 | $6.10 | $0.50 | $0.10 | $0.60 |
| $1.20 | $5.70 | $6.20 | $0.50 | $0.20 | $0.70 |

## Question 4.14

Hedging should never be thought of as a profit increasing action. A company that hedges merely shifts profits from good to bad states of the relevant price risk that the hedge seeks to diminish.

The value of the reduced profits, should the gold price rise, subsidizes the payment to Golddiggers should the gold price fall. Therefore, a company may use a hedge for one of the reasons stated in the textbook; however, it is not correct to compare hedged and unhedged companies from an accounting perspective.

## Question 4.16

a) Expected pre-tax profit

Firm A: E[Profit] = $0.5 \times (\$1,000) + 0.5 \times (-\$600) = \$200$

Firm B: E[Profit] = $0.5 \times (\$300) + 0.5 \times (\$100) = \$200$

Both firms have the same pre-tax profit.

b) Expected after tax profit. Firm A:

|  | | Bad state | Good state |
|---|---|---|---|
| (1) | Pre-Tax Operating Income | −$600 | $1,000 |
| (2) | Taxable Income | $0 | $1,000 |
| (3) | Tax @ 40% | 0 | $400 |
| (3b) | Tax Credit | $240 | 0 |
|  | After-Tax Income (including Tax credit) | −$360 | $600 |

This gives an expected after-tax profit for firm A of:

$$E[\text{Profit}] = 0.5 \times (-\$360) + 0.5 \times (\$600) = \$120$$

Firm B:

|  | | Bad state | Good state |
|---|---|---|---|
| (1) | Pre-Tax Operating Income | $100 | $300 |
| (2) | Taxable Income | $100 | $300 |
| (3) | Tax @ 40% | $40 | $120 |
| (3b) | Tax Credit | 0 | 0 |
|  | After-Tax Income (including Tax credit) | $60 | $180 |

This gives an expected after-tax profit for firm B of:

$$E[\text{Profit}] = 0.5 \times (\$60) + 0.5 \times (\$180) = \$120$$

If firms receive full credit for tax losses, the tax code does not have an effect on the expected after-tax profits of firms that have the same expected pre-tax profits but different cash-flow variability.

# Question 4.18

Auric Enterprises is using gold as an input. Therefore, it would like to hedge against price increases in gold.

a) The cost of this collar today is the premium of the purchased 440-strike call ($2.49) less the premium for the sold 400-strike put. We calculate a cost of $2.49 − $2.21 = −$0.28, which means that Auric in fact generates a revenue from entering into this collar.

b) The values of part (a) are a good starting point. You see that both put and call are worth approximately the same; therefore, start shrinking the 440 − 400 span symmetrically until you get a difference of 30 and then do some trial and error. This should bring you the following values: The call strike is 435.52, and the put strike is 405.52. Both call and put have a premium of $3.425.

# Question 4.20

a) Since we know that the value of a call is decreasing in the strike and we need to sell two call options, the Black-Scholes prices that equal the 440-strike call price, we know that we have to look for a higher strike price. Trial and error results in a strike price of 448.93. The premium of the 440-strike call is $2.4944, and indeed the Black-Scholes premium of the 448.93 strike call is $1.2472.

b) Profit diagram:

## Question 4.22

a) We have the following table:

| Price | Quantity | Revenue |
|-------|----------|---------|
| 3 | 1.5 | 4.5 |
| 3 | 0.8 | 2.4 |
| 2 | 1 | 2 |
| 2 | 0.6 | 1.2 |

Using Excel's function STDEVP(4.5,2.4,2,1.2), we obtain a value of 1.2194 for the standard deviation of total revenue for Scenario C.

b) Using any standard software's command (or doing it by hand!) to determine the correlation coefficient, we obtain a value of 0.7586.

## Question 4.24

a) The expected quantity of production is $0.25 \times (1.5 + 0.8 + 1 + 0.6) = 0.975$ million bushels of corn.

b)

| Price | Quantity | Unhedged revenue | Futures gain from shorting 0.975m contracts | Total |
|-------|----------|------------------|---------------------------------------------|-------|
| 3 | 1.5m | 4.5m | $-0.5 \times 0.975m$ $= -0.4875m$ | 4.0125m |
| 3 | 0.8m | 2.4m | $-0.5 \times 0.975m$ $= -0.4875m$ | 1.9125m |
| 2 | 1m | 2m | $0.5 \times 0.975m$ $= 0.4875m$ | 2.4875m |
| 2 | 0.6m | 1.2m | $0.5 \times 0.975m$ $= 0.4875m$ | 1.6875m |

Using Excel's function STDEVP(4.0125, 1.9125, 2.4875, 1.6875), we obtain a value of 0.907004 for the standard deviation of the optimally hedged revenue for Scenario C. We see that we were able to reduce the variance of our revenues, albeit to a lesser degree than with the optimally hedged portfolio.

# Chapter 5

## Financial Forwards and Futures

### Question 5.2

a) The owner of the stock is entitled to receive dividends. As we will get the stock only in one year, the value of the prepaid forward contract is today's stock price, less the present value of the four dividend payments:

$$F_{0,T}^P = \$50 - \sum_{i=1}^{4} \$1 e^{-0.06 \times \frac{3}{12} i} = \$50 - \$0.985 - \$0.970 - \$0.956 - \$0.942$$

$$= \$50 - \$3.853 = \$46.147$$

b) The forward price is equivalent to the future value of the prepaid forward. With an interest rate of 6 percent and an expiration of the forward in one year, we thus have:

$$F_{0,T} = F_{0,T}^P \times e^{0.06 \times 1} = \$46.147 \times e^{0.06 \times 1} = \$46.147 \times 1.0618 = \$49.00$$

### Question 5.4

This question asks us to familiarize ourselves with the forward valuation equation.

a) We plug the continuously compounded interest rate and the time to expiration in years into the valuation formula and notice that the time to expiration is six months, or 0.5 years. We have:

$$F_{0,T} = S_0 \times e^{r \times T} = \$35 \times e^{0.05 \times 0.5} = \$35 \times 1.0253 = \$35.886$$

b) The annualized forward premium is calculated as:

$$\text{annualized forward premium} = \frac{1}{T} \ln\left(\frac{F_{0,T}}{S_0}\right) = \frac{1}{0.5} \ln\left(\frac{\$35.50}{\$35}\right) = 0.0284$$

c) For the case of continuous dividends, the forward premium is simply the difference between the risk-free rate and the dividend yield:

$$\text{annualized forward premium} = \frac{1}{T} \ln\left(\frac{F_{0,T}}{S_0}\right) = \frac{1}{T} \ln\left(\frac{S_0 \times e^{(r-\delta)T}}{S_0}\right)$$

$$= \frac{1}{T} \ln\left(e^{(r-\delta)T}\right) = \frac{1}{T}(r-\delta)T$$

$$= r - \delta$$

Therefore, we can solve:

$$0.0284 = 0.05 - \delta$$
$$\Leftrightarrow \delta \quad = 0.0216$$

The annualized dividend yield is 2.16 percent.

# Question 5.6

a) We plug the continuously compounded interest rate, the dividend yield and the time to expiration in years into the valuation formula and notice that the time to expiration is nine months, or 0.75 years. We have:

$$F_{0,T} = S_0 \times e^{(r-\delta)\times T} = \$1,100 \times e^{(0.05-0.015)\times 0.75} = \$1,100 \times 1.0266 = \$1,129.26$$

b) We engage in a reverse cash and carry strategy. In particular, we do the following:

| Description | Today | In nine months |
|---|---|---|
| Long forward, resulting from customer purchase | 0 | $S_T - F_{0,T}$ |
| Sell short tailed position of the index | $+S_0 e^{-\delta T}$ | $-S_T$ |
| Lend $S_0 e^{-\delta T}$ | $-S_0 e^{-\delta T}$ | $S_0 \times e^{(r-\delta)T}$ |
| TOTAL | 0 | $S_0 \times e^{(r-\delta)T} - F_{0,T}$ |

Specifically, we have:

| Description | Today | In nine months |
|---|---|---|
| Long forward, resulting from customer purchase | 0 | $S_T - \$1,129.26$ |
| Sell short tailed position of the index | $\$1,100 \times 0.9888 = 1087.69$ | $-S_T$ |
| Lend $1,087.69 | $-\$1,087.69$ | $\$1,087.69 \times e^{0.05\times 0.75} = \$1,129.26$ |
| TOTAL | 0 | 0 |

Therefore, the market maker is perfectly hedged. He does not have any risk in the future, because he has successfully created a synthetic short position in the forward contract.

c)

| Description | Today | In nine months |
|---|---|---|
| Short forward, resulting from customer purchase | 0 | $F_{0,T} - S_T$ |
| Buy tailed position in index | $-S_0 e^{-\delta T}$ | $S_T$ |
| Borrow $S_0 e^{-\delta T}$ | $S_0 e^{-\delta T}$ | $-S_0 \times e^{(r-\delta)T}$ |
| TOTAL | 0 | $F_{0,T} - S_0 \times e^{(r-\delta)T}$ |

Specifically, we have:

| Description | Today | In nine months |
|---|---|---|
| Short forward, resulting from customer purchase | 0 | $\$1,129.26 - S_T$ |
| Buy tailed position in index | $-\$1,100 \times 0.9888$ $= -\$1,087.69$ | $S_T$ |
| Borrow $ 1,087.69 | $\$1,087.69$ | $-\$1,087.69 \times e^{0.05 \times 0.75}$ $= -\$1,129.26$ |
| TOTAL | 0 | 0 |

Again, the market maker is perfectly hedged. He does not have any index price risk in the future, because he has successfully created a synthetic long position in the forward contract that perfectly offsets his obligation from the sold forward contract.

## Question 5.8

First, we need to find the fair value of the forward price. We plug the continuously compounded interest rate, the dividend yield and the time to expiration in years into the valuation formula and notice that the time to expiration is six months, or 0.5 years. We have:

$$F_{0,T} = S_0 \times e^{(r-\delta) \times T} = \$1,100 \times e^{(0.05-0.02) \times 0.5} = \$1,100 \times 1.01511 = \$1,116.62$$

a) If we observe a forward price of $1,120, we know that the forward is too expensive, relative to the fair value we have determined. Therefore, we will sell the forward at $1,120, and create a synthetic forward for $1,116.82, making a sure profit of $3.38. As we sell the real forward, we engage in cash and carry arbitrage:

| Description | Today | In six months |
|---|---|---|
| Short forward | 0 | $1,120.00 − S_T$ |
| Buy tailed position in index | −$1,100 × .99 = −$1,089.055 | $S_T$ |
| Borrow $1,089.055 | $1,089.055 | −$1,116.62 |
| TOTAL | 0 | $3.38 |

This position requires no initial investment, has no index price risk, and has a strictly positive payoff. We have exploited the mispricing with a pure arbitrage strategy.

b) If we observe a forward price of $1,110, we know that the forward is too cheap, relative to the fair value we have determined. Therefore, we will buy the forward at $1,110, and create a synthetic short forward for $1,116.62, thus making a sure profit of $6.62. As we buy the real forward, we engage in a reverse cash and carry arbitrage:

| Description | Today | In six months |
|---|---|---|
| Long forward | 0 | $S_T − \$1,110.00$ |
| Sell short tailed position in index | $1,100 × .99 = $1,089.055 | $−S_T$ |
| Lend $1,089.055 | −$1,089.055 | $1,116.62 |
| TOTAL | 0 | $6.62 |

This position requires no initial investment, has no index price risk, and has a strictly positive payoff. We have exploited the mispricing with a pure arbitrage strategy.

## Question 5.10

a) We plug the continuously compounded interest rate, the forward price, the initial index level and the time to expiration in years into the valuation formula and solve for the dividend yield:

$$F_{0,T} = S_0 \times e^{(r - \delta) \times T}$$

$$\Leftrightarrow \quad \frac{F_{0,T}}{S_0} = e^{(r - \delta) \times T}$$

$$\Leftrightarrow \quad \ln\left(\frac{F_{0,T}}{S_0}\right) = (r - \delta) \times T$$

$$\Leftrightarrow \quad \delta = r - \frac{1}{T}\ln\left(\frac{F_{0,T}}{S_0}\right)$$

$$\Rightarrow \quad \delta = 0.05 - \frac{1}{0.75}\ln\left(\frac{1129.257}{1100}\right) = 0.05 - 0.035 = 0.015$$

Remark: Note that this result is consistent with exercise 5.6., in which we had the same forward prices, time to expiration etc.

b) With a dividend yield of only 0.005, the fair forward price would be:

$$F_{0,T} = S_0 \times e^{(r-\delta)\times T} = 1{,}100 \times e^{(0.05-0.005)\times0.75} = 1{,}100 \times 1.0343 = 1{,}137.759$$

Therefore, if we think the dividend yield is 0.005, we consider the observed forward price of \$1,129.257 to be too cheap. We will therefore buy the forward and create a synthetic short forward, capturing a certain amount of \$8.502. We engage in a reverse cash and carry arbitrage:

| Description | Today | In nine months |
|---|---|---|
| Long forward | 0 | $S_T - \$1{,}129.257$ |
| Sell short tailed position in | $\$1{,}100 \times 0.99626$ | $-S_T$ |
| index | $= \$1{,}095.88$ | |
| Lend \$1,095.88 | $-\$1{,}095.88$ | \$1,137.759 |
| TOTAL | 0 | \$8.502 |

c) With a dividend yield of 0.03, the fair forward price would be:

$$F_{0,T} = S_0 \times e^{(r-\delta)\times T} = 1{,}100 \times e^{(0.05-0.03)\times0.75} = 1{,}100 \times 1.01511 = 1{,}116.62$$

Therefore, if we think the dividend yield is 0.03, we consider the observed forward price of \$1,129.257 to be too expensive. We will therefore sell the forward and create a synthetic long forward, capturing a certain amount of \$12.637. We engage in a cash and carry arbitrage:

| Description | Today | In nine months |
|---|---|---|
| Short forward | 0 | $\$1{,}129.257 - S_T$ |
| Buy tailed position in | $-\$1{,}100 \times .97775$ | $S_T$ |
| index | $= -\$1{,}075.526$ | |
| Borrow \$1,075.526 | \$1,075.526 | \$1,116.62 |
| TOTAL | 0 | \$12.637 |

## Question 5.12

a) The notional value of 10 contracts is $10 \times \$250 \times 950 = \$2,375,000$, because each index point is worth \$250, we buy 10 contracts and the S&P 500 index level is 950.

With an initial margin of 10 percent of the notional value, this results in an initial dollar margin of:

$$\$2,375,000 \times 0.10 = \$237,500.$$

b) We first obtain an approximation. Because we have a 10 percent initial margin, a 2 percent decline in the futures price will result in a 20 percent decline in margin. As we will receive a margin call after a 20 percent decline in the initial margin, the smallest futures price that avoids the maintenance margin call is $950 \times 0.98 = 931$. However, this calculation ignores the interest that we are able to earn in our margin account.

Let us now calculate the details. We have the right to earn interest on our initial margin position. As the continuously compounded interest rate is currently 6 percent, after one week, our initial margin has grown to:

$$\$237,500 e^{0.06 \times \frac{1}{52}} = \$237,774.20$$

We will get a margin call if the initial margin falls by 20 percent. We calculate 80 percent of the initial margin as:

$$\$237,500 \times 0.8 = \$190,000$$

Ten long S&P 500 futures contracts obligate us to pay \$2,500 times the forward price at expiration of the futures contract.

Therefore, we have to solve the following equation:

$$
\begin{aligned}
\$237,774.20 + (F_{1W} - 950) \times \$2,500 &\geq \$190,000 \\
\Leftrightarrow \quad \$47774.20 &\geq -(F_{1W} - 950) \times \$2,500 \\
\Leftrightarrow \quad 19.10968 - 950 &\geq -F_{1W} \\
\Leftrightarrow \quad F_{1W} &\geq 930.89
\end{aligned}
$$

Therefore, the greatest S&P 500 index futures price at which we will receive a margin call is 930.88.

## Question 5.14

An arbitrageur believing that the observed forward price, $F(0,T)$, is too low will undertake a reverse cash and carry arbitrage: buy the forward, short sell the stock, and lend out the proceeds from the short sale. The relevant prices are, therefore, the bid price of the stock and the lending interest rate. Also, she will incur the transaction costs twice. We have:

| Description | Today | In nine months |
|---|---|---|
| Long forward | 0 | $S_T - F_{0,T}$ |
| Sell short tailed position of the index | $+S_b\,e^{-\delta T}$ | $-S_T$ |
| Pay twice transaction cost | $-2 \times k$ | |
| Lend $S_0^b e^{-\delta T} - 2\times k$ | $-S_0^b e^{-\delta T} + 2\times k$ | $(+S_0^b e^{-\delta T} - 2\times k) \times e^{r^l T}$ |
| TOTAL | 0 | $(+S_0^b e^{-\delta T} - 2\times k) \times e^{r^l T} - F_{0,T}$ |

To avoid arbitrage, we must have $\left(S_0^b e^{-\delta T} - 2\times k\right) \times e^{r^l T} - F_{0,T} \leq 0$. This is equivalent to $F_{0,T} \geq \left(S_0^b e^{-\delta T} - 2\times k\right) \times e^{r^l T}$. Therefore, for any $F_{0,T}$ smaller than this bound, there exist arbitrage opportunities.

## Question 5.16

a)  The one-year futures price is determined as:
$$F_{0,1} = 875e^{0.0475} = 875 \times 1.048646 = 917.57$$

b)  One futures contract has the value of $250 \times 875 = \$218,750$. Therefore, the number of contracts needed to cover the exposure of $800,000 is: $800,000 \div \$218,750 = 3.65714$. Furthermore, we need to adjust for the difference in beta. Since the beta of our portfolio exceeds 1, it moves more than the index in either direction. Therefore, we must increase the number of contracts. The final hedge quantity is: $3.65714 \times 1.1 = 4.02286$. Therefore, we should short sell 4.02286 S&P 500 index future contracts.

As the correlation between the index and our portfolio is assumed to be one, we have no basis risk and have perfectly hedged our position and transformed it into a riskless investment. Therefore, we expect to earn the risk-free interest rate as a return over one year.

## Question 5.18

The current exchange rate is 0.02E/Y, which implies 50Y/E. The euro continuously compounded interest rate is 0.04, the yen continuously compounded interest rate 0.01. Time to expiration is 0.5 years. Plug the input variables into the formula to see that:

$$\text{Euro/Yen forward} = 0.02e^{(0.04-0.01)\times0.5} = 0.02 \times 1.015113 = 0.020302$$
$$\text{Yen/Euro forward} = 50e^{(0.01-0.04)\times0.5} = 50 \times 0.98511 = 49.2556$$

## Question 5.20

a)  The Eurodollar futures price is 93.23. Therefore, we can use equation (5.20) of the main text to back out the three-month LIBOR rate:

$$r_{91} = (100 - 93.23) \times \frac{1}{100} \times \frac{1}{4} \times \frac{91}{90} = 0.017113.$$

b)  We will have to repay principal plus interest on the loan that we are taking from the following June to September. Because we shorted a Eurodollar futures, we are guaranteed the interest rate we calculated in part (a). Therefore, we have a repayment of:

$$\$10,000,000 \times (1 + r_{91}) = \$10,000,000 \times 1.017113 = \$10,171,130$$

# Chapter 6

## Commodity Forwards and Futures

### Question 6.2

The spot price of oil is $32.00 per barrel. With a continuously compounded annual risk-free rate of 2 percent, we can again calculate the lease rate according to the formula:

$$\delta_l = r - \frac{1}{T}\ln\left(\frac{F_{0,T}}{S_0}\right)$$

| Time to expiration | Forward price | Annualized lease rate |
|---|---|---|
| 3 months | $31.37 | 0.0995355 |
| 6 months | $30.75 | 0.0996918 |
| 9 months | $30.14 | 0.0998436 |
| 12 months | $29.54 | 0.0999906 |

The lease rate is higher than the risk-free interest rate. The forward curve is downward sloping, thus the prices of exercise 6.2 are an example of backwardation.

### Question 6.4

a) As we need to borrow a pound of copper to sell it short, we must pay the lender the lease rate for the time we borrow the asset, i.e., until expiration of the contract in one year. After one year, we have to pay back one pound of copper, which will cost us $S_T$, the uncertain future pound of copper price, plus the leasing costs: Total payment $= S_T + S_T \times e^{0.05} - 1 = S_T\, e^{0.05} = 1.05127 \times S_T$.

It does not make sense to store a pound of copper in equilibrium, because even if we have an active lease market for pounds of copper, the lease rate is smaller than the risk-free interest rate. Lending money at 10 percent is more profitable than lending pounds of copper at 5 percent.

b) The equilibrium forward price is calculated according to our pricing formula:

$$F_{0,T} = S_0 \times e^{(r-\delta_l)\times T} = \$3.00 \times e^{(0.10-0.05)\times 1} = \$3.00 \times 1.05127 = \$3.1538,$$

which is the price given in the exercise.

c) Copper need not be stored because there is a constant supply of copper. If the forward price was greater than 3.316, then a copper producer will find it profitable to sell forward production.

d) As the textbook points out, the reverse cash-and-carry arbitrage does not put a lower bound on the forward price. The lender will require a lease payment and can use the forward price to determine the lease rate.

## Question 6.6

a) The forward prices reflect a market for widgets in which seasonality is important. Let us look at two examples, one with constant demand and seasonal supply, and another one with constant supply and seasonal demand.

One possible explanation might be that widgets are extremely difficult to produce and that they need one key ingredient that is only available during July/August. However, the demand for the widget is constant throughout the year. In order to be able to sell the widgets throughout the year, widgets must be stored after production in August. The forward curve reflects the ever increasing storage costs of widgets until the next production cycle arrives. Once produced, widget prices fall again to the spot price.

Another story that is consistent with the observed prices of widgets is that widgets are in particularly high demand during the summer months. The storage of widgets may be costly, which means that widget producers are reluctant to build up inventory long before the summer. Storage occurs slowly over the winter months and inventories build up sharply just before the highest demand during the summer months. The forward prices reflect those storage cycle costs.

b) Let us take the December Year 0 forward price as a proxy for the spot price in December Year 0. We can then calculate with our cash and carry arbitrage tableau:

| Transaction | Time 0 | Time $T = 3/12$ |
|---|---|---|
| Short March forward | 0 | $3.075 - S_T$ |
| Buy December | $-3.00$ | $S_T$ |
| Forward (= Buy spot) | | |
| Pay storage cost | $-0.03$ | |
| Total | $-3.00$ | $3.045$ |

We can calculate the annualized rate of return as:

$$\frac{3.045}{3.00} = e^{(r) \times T}$$

$$\Leftrightarrow \ln\left(\frac{3.045}{3.00}\right) = r \times 3/12$$

$$r = 0.05955$$

which is the prevailing risk-free interest rate of 0.06. This result seems to make sense.

c) Let us again take the December Year 0 forward price as a proxy for the spot price in December Year 0. We can then calculate with our cash and carry arbitrage tableau:

| Transaction | Time 0 | Time $T= 9/12$ |
|---|---|---|
| Short Sep forward | 0 | $2.75 - S_T$ |
| Buy spot | −3.00 | $S_T$ |
| Pay storage cost Sep | | −0.03 |
| FV(Storage Jun) | | −0.0305 |
| FV(Storage Mar) | −0.0309 | |
| Total | −3.00 | 2.6586 |

We can calculate the annualized rate of return as:

$$\frac{2.6586}{3.00} = e^{(r)\times T} \Leftrightarrow \ln\left(\frac{2.6586}{3.00}\right) = r \times 9/12$$

$$r = -0.16108$$

This result does not seem to make sense. We would earn a negative annualized return of 16 percent on such a cash and carry arbitrage. Therefore, it is likely that our naive calculations do not capture an important fact about the widget market. In particular, we will buy and hold the widget through a time where the forward curve indicates that there is a significant convenience yield attached to widgets.

It is tempting, although premature, to conclude that a reverse cash and carry arbitrage may make a positive 16 percent annualized return. Question 6.7 deals with this aspect.

## Question 6.8

a) The first possibility is a simple cash and carry arbitrage:

| Transaction | Time 0 | Time $T= 3/12$ |
|---|---|---|
| Short March forward | 0 | $3.10 - S_T$ |
| Buy December forward (= Buy spot) | −3.00 | $S_T$ |
| Borrow @ 6% | +3.00 | −3.045 |
| Pay storage cost | −0.03 | |
| Total | 0 | +0.025 |

The second possibility involves using the June futures contract. It is a forward cash-and-carry strategy:

| Transaction | Time = $T(1) = 3/12$ | Time = $T(2) = 6/12$ |
|---|---|---|
| Short March forward | $3.10 - S_{T(1)}$ | $-S_{T(2)}$ |
| Buy June forward | 0 | $S_{T(2)} - 3.152$ |
| Lend @ 6% | $-3.10$ | 3.1469 |
| Receive storage cost | | $+0.03$ |
| Total | 0 | $+0.02485$ |

We can use the June futures in our calculations and claim to receive storage costs because it is easy to show that the value of it is reflecting the negative lease rate of the storage costs.

b) It is not possible to undertake an arbitrage with the futures contracts that expire prior to September Year 1. A decrease in the September futures value means that we would need to buy the September futures contract, and any arbitrage strategy would need some short position in the widget. However, the drop in the futures price in September indicates that there is a significant convenience yield factored into the futures price over the period June–September. As we have no information about it, it is not possible for us to guarantee that we will find a lender of widgets at a favorable lease rate to follow through our arbitrage trading program. The decrease in the September futures may in fact reflect an increase in the opportunity costs of widget owners.

## Question 6.10

Our best bet for the current spot price is the first available forward price, properly discounted by taking the interest rate and the lease rate into account, and by ignoring any storage cost and convenience yield (because we do not have any information on it):

$$F_{0,T} = S_0 \times e^{(r - \delta_l) \times T}$$
$$\Leftrightarrow S_0 = F_{0,T} \times e^{-(r - \delta_l) \times T}$$
$$\Leftrightarrow S_0 = 313.81 \times e^{-(0.06 - 0.015) \times 1} = 313.81 \times 0.956 = 300.0016$$

## Question 6.12

a) Widgets do not deteriorate over time and are costless to store; therefore, the lender does not save anything by lending me the widget. On the other hand, there is a constant demand and flexible production—there is no seasonality. Therefore, we should expect that the convenience yield is very close to the risk-free rate, merely compensating the lender for the opportunity cost.

b)  Demand varies seasonally, but the production process is flexible. Therefore, we would expect that producers anticipate the seasonality in demand, and adjust production accordingly. Again, the lease rate should not be much higher than the risk-free rate.

c)  Now we have the problem that the demand for widgets will spike up without an appropriate adjustment of production. Let us suppose that widget demand is high in June, July, and August. Then, we will face a substantial lease rate if we were to borrow the widget in May and return it in September: We would deprive the merchant of the widget when he would need it most (and could probably earn a significant amount of money on it), and we would return it when the season is over. We most likely pay a substantial lease rate.

On the other hand, suppose we want to borrow the widget in January and return it in June. Now we return the widget precisely when the merchant needs it and have it over a time where demand is low, and he is not likely to sell it. The lease rate is likely to be very small.

However, those stylized facts are weakened by the fact that the merchant can costlessly store widgets, so the smart merchant has a larger inventory when demand is high, offsetting the above effects at a substantial amount.

d)  Suppose that production is very low during June, July, and August. Let us think about borrowing the widget in May and returning it in September. We do again deprive the merchant of the widget when he needs it most, because with a constant demand, less production means widgets become a comparably scarce resource and increase in price. Therefore, we pay a higher lease rate. The opposite effects can be observed for a widget-borrowing from January to June.

Again, these stylized facts are offset by the above mentioned inventory considerations.

e)  If widgets cannot be stored, the seasonality problems become very severe, leading to larger swings in the lease rate due to the impossibility of managing inventory.

# Chapter 7

## Interest Rate Forwards and Futures

### Question 7.2

The coupon bond pays a coupon of $60 each year plus the principal of $1,000 after five years. We have cash flows of [60, 60, 60, 60, 1,060]. To obtain the price of the coupon bond, we multiply each cash flow by the zero-coupon bond price of that year. This yields a bond price of $1,037.25280.

### Question 7.4

| Maturity | Zero-Coupon Bond Yield | Zero-Coupon Bond Price | One-Year Implied Forward Rate | Par Coupon | Cont. Comp. Zero Yield |
|---|---|---|---|---|---|
| 1 | 0.05000 | 0.95238 | 0.05000 | 0.05000 | 0.04879 |
| 2 | 0.04200 | 0.92101 | 0.03406 | 0.04216 | 0.04114 |
| 3 | 0.04000 | 0.88900 | 0.03601 | 0.04018 | 0.03922 |
| 4 | 0.03600 | 0.86808 | 0.02409 | 0.03634 | 0.03537 |
| 5 | 0.02900 | 0.86681 | 0.00147 | 0.02962 | 0.02859 |

### Question 7.6

In order to be able to solve this problem, it is best to take equation (7.6) of the main text and solve progressively for all zero-coupon bond prices, starting with Year 1. This yields the series of zero-coupon bond prices from which we can proceed as usual to determine the yields.

| Maturity | Zero-Coupon Bond Yield | Zero-Coupon Bond Price | One-Year Implied Forward Rate | Par Coupon | Cont. Comp. Zero Yield |
|---|---|---|---|---|---|
| 1 | 0.03000 | 0.97087 | 0.03000 | 0.03000 | 0.02956 |
| 2 | 0.03500 | 0.93352 | 0.04002 | 0.03491 | 0.03440 |
| 3 | 0.04000 | 0.88899 | 0.05009 | 0.03974 | 0.03922 |
| 4 | 0.04700 | 0.83217 | 0.06828 | 0.04629 | 0.04593 |
| 5 | 0.05300 | 0.77245 | 0.07732 | 0.05174 | 0.05164 |

## Question 7.8

a) We have to take into account the interest we (or our counterparty) can earn on the FRA settlement if we settle the loan on initiation day and not on the actual repayment day. Therefore, we tail the FRA settlement by the prevailing market interest rate of 5 percent. The dollar settlement is:

$$\frac{\left(r_{annually} - r_{FRA}\right)}{1 + r_{annually}} \times \text{notional principal} = \frac{(0.05 - 0.06)}{1 + 0.05} \times \$500,000.00 = -\$4,761.905$$

b) If the FRA is settled on the date the loan is repaid (or settled in arrears), the settlement amount is determined by:

$$\left(r_{annually} - r_{FRA}\right) \times \text{notional principal} = (0.05 - 0.06) \times \$500,000.00 = -\$5,000$$

We have to pay at the settlement because the interest rate we could borrow at is 5 percent, but we have agreed via the FRA to a borrowing rate of 6 percent. Interest rates moved in an unfavorable direction.

## Question 7.10

We can find the implied forward rates using the following formula:

$$\left[1 + r_0\left(t, t = s\right)\right] = \frac{P_0\left(0, t\right)}{P\left(0, t + s\right)}$$

This yields the following rates on the synthetic FRAs:

$$r_0\left(90, 180\right) = \frac{0.99009}{0.97943} - 1 = 0.010884$$

$$r_0\left(90, 270\right) = \frac{0.99009}{0.96525} - 1 = 0.025734$$

$$r_0\left(90, 360\right) = \frac{0.99009}{0.95238} - 1 = 0.039596$$

## Question 7.12

We can find the implied forward rate using the following formula:

$$\left[1 + r_0\left(t, t = s\right)\right] = \frac{P_0\left(0, t\right)}{P\left(0, t + s\right)}$$

With the numbers of the exercise, this yields:

$$r_0\left(270, 360\right) = \frac{0.96525}{0.95238} - 1 = 0.0135135$$

The following table follows the textbook in looking at forward agreements from a borrower's perspective (i.e., a borrower goes long on an FRA to hedge his position and a lender is thus short the FRA). Since we are the counterparty for a lender, we are in fact the borrower and thus long the forward rate agreement.

| Transaction today | $t = 0$ | $t = 270$ | $t = 360$ |
|---|---|---|---|
| Enter long FRA | | 10M | $-10M \times 1.013514$ |
| | | | $= -10.13514M$ |
| Sell 9.6525M Zero Coupons maturing at time $t = 180$ | 9.6525M | −10M | |
| Buy $(1 + 0.013514) * 10M * 0.95238$ | $-10M \times 1.013514$ | | $+10.13514M$ |
| Zero Coupons maturing at time $t = 360$ | $\times 0.95238 = -9.6525M$ | | |
| TOTAL | 0 | 0 | 0 |

By entering in the above mentioned positions, we are perfectly hedged against the risk of the FRA. Please note that we are making use of the fact that interest rates are perfectly predictable.

## Question 7.14

We would like to guarantee the return of 6.5 percent. We receive payments 6.95485 after Year 1 and Year 2, and a payment of 106.95485 after Year 3. If interest rates are uncertain, we face an interest rate risk for the investment of the first coupon from Year 1 to Year 2 and for the discounting of the final payment from Year 3 to Year 1.

Suppose we enter into a forward rate agreement to lend 6.95484 from Year 1 to Year 2 at the current forward rate from Year 1 to Year 2, and we enter into a forward rate agreement to borrow 106.95485 tailed by the prevailing forward rate for Year 2 to Year 3, at the prevailing forward rate. This leads to the following cash-flow table:

| Transaction today | $t = 0$ | $t = 1$ | $t = 2$ | $t = 3$ |
|---|---|---|---|---|
| Buy three-year par bond | −100 | | | |
| Receive first coupon | 0 | 6.95485 | | |
| Enter short FRA | 0 | −6.95485 | 6.95485 × 1.0700237 | |
| Receive second coupon | 0 | | 6.95485 | |
| Enter long FRA for tailed position | 0 | | 106.95485/1.0800705 | −106.95485 |
| Receive final coupon and principal | 0 | | = 99.025804 | 106.95485 |
| TOTAL | −100 | 0 | 113.4225 | 0 |

We see that we can secure the same gross return as in the previous question, $\sqrt{113.4225 \div 100}$ = 1.065. By entering appropriate FRAs, we secured the desired return of 6.5 percent. Please note that we made use of the fact that we knew that we wanted to undo the position at $t = 2$.

## Question 7.16

a) The implied LIBOR of the September Eurodollar futures of 96.4 is: $\dfrac{100 - 96.4}{400} = 0.9\%$

b) As we want to borrow money, we want to buy protection against high interest rates, which means low Eurodollar future prices. We will short the Eurodollar contract.

c) One Eurodollar contract is based on a $1 million three-month deposit. As we want to hedge a loan of $50M, we will enter into 50 short contracts.

d) A true three-month LIBOR of 1 percent means an annualized position (annualized by market conventions) of 1% ∗ 4 = 4%. Therefore, our 50 short contracts will pay:

$$[96.4 - (100 - 4) \times 100 \times \$25 \times 50] = \$50,000$$

The increase in the interest rate has made our loan more expensive. The futures position that we entered to hedge the interest rate exposure compensates for this increase. In particular, we pay $50,000,000 × 0.01 − *payoff futures* = $500,000 − $50,000 = $450,000, which corresponds to the 0.9 percent we sought to lock in.

## Question 7.18

a) We face the classic problem of asset mismatch. We are interested in locking in an interest rate for a 150-day investment, 60 days from now. However, while the Eurodollar futures matures 60 days from now, it secures a lending rate for 90 days. We face the problem that the 90-day and 150-day interest rates may not be perfectly correlated. (For example, the term structure could, over the next 60 days, move from upward sloping to downward sloping).

b) As we want to lend money, we want to buy protection against low interest rates, which means high Eurodollar future prices. We will therefore long the Eurodollar contract.

c) The implied LIBOR of the September Eurodollar futures of 94 is: $\dfrac{100-94}{400} = 1.5$ percent.

Under the assumption that the three-month LIBOR rate and the 150-day interest rate are based on the same annualized interest rate of 6 percent, we are able to lock in an interest rate of: $1.5\% \times \dfrac{150}{90} = 2.5$ percent. Please note that this is a rather strong assumption.

d) One Eurodollar futures contract is based on a $1 million three-month deposit. As we want to hedge an investment of $100M, we will enter into 100 long contracts. Again, we are making the strong assumption that the annualized three-month LIBOR rate and the annualized 150 day rate are identical and perfectly correlated.

## Question 7.20

We will use the Excel functions Duration and Mduration to calculate the required durations. They are of the form:

$$\text{MDURATION(Start Date; Terminal Date; Coupon; Yield; Frequency)}$$

$$\text{DURATION(Start Date; Terminal Date; Coupon; Yield; Frequency),}$$

where frequency determines the number of coupon payments per year. In order to use the function, we have to give Excel a start date and terminal date, but we can just pick two dates that are exactly the requested number of years apart. Plugging in the values of the exercises yields:

a) Macaulay Duration = 4.59324084

Modified Duration = 4.3983078

b) Macaulay Duration = 5.99377496

Modified Duration = 5.73566981

c) We need to find the yield to maturity of this bond first. We can do so by using the YIELD function of Excel. Plugging in the relevant values, we get: Yield = 0.07146759. Now we can again use the Mduration and Duration formulas. This yields:

Macaulay Duration = 7.6955970

Modified Duration = 7.1822957

## Question 7.22

We will exploit equation (7.13) of the main text to find the optimal hedge ratio:

$$N = -\frac{D_1 B_1\left(y_1\right)/\left(1+y_1\right)}{D_2 B_2\left(y_2\right)/\left(1+y_2\right)} = \frac{6.631864 \times 106.44/\left(1.05004\right)}{7.098302 \times 112.29/\left(1.05252\right)} = -\frac{672.255918}{757.2951883} = -0.887707$$

Therefore, we have to short 0.887707 units of the nine-year bond for every eight-year bond to obtain a duration-matched portfolio.

## Question 7.24

a) Compute the convexity of a three-year bond paying annual coupons of 4.5 percent and selling at par. For a par bond, the yield to maturity is equal to the coupon, or 4.5 percent in our case. We can calculate the convexity based on the formula:

$$\text{Convexity} = \frac{1}{B_y}\left[\sum_{i=1}^{n} \frac{i(i+1)}{m^2} \frac{C/m}{(1+y/m)^{i+2}} + \frac{n(n+1)}{m^2} \frac{M}{(1+y/m)^{n+2}}\right]$$

$$= \frac{1}{100}\left[\frac{1(1+1)}{1^2} \frac{4.5/1}{(1+0.045)^{1+2}} + \frac{2(2+1)}{1^2} \frac{4.5/1}{(1+0.045)^{2+2}}\right.$$

$$\left. + \frac{3(3+1)}{1^2} \frac{104.5}{(1+0.045/1)^{3+2}}\right]$$

$$= 10.3680$$

b) Compute the convexity of a three-year 4.5 percent coupon bond that makes semiannual coupon payments and that currently sells at par.

Now, $m = 2$. We have $n = m * T = 2 * 3 = 6$. The convexity is:

$$\text{Convexity} = \frac{1}{B_y}\left[\sum_{i=1}^{n} \frac{i(i+1)}{m^2} \frac{C/m}{(1+y/m)^{i+2}} + \frac{n(n+1)}{m^2} \frac{M}{(1+y/m)^{n+2}}\right]$$

$$= \frac{1}{100}\left[\frac{1(1+1)}{2^2} \frac{2.25/1}{(1+0.0225)^{1+2}} + \frac{2(2+1)}{2^2} \frac{2.25/1}{(1+0.0225)^{2+2}}\right.$$

$$+ \frac{3(3+1)}{2^2} \frac{2.25/1}{(1+0.0225/1)^{3+2}} + \frac{4(4+1)}{2^2} \frac{2.25/1}{(1+0.0225/1)^{4+2}}$$

$$\left. + \frac{5(5+1)}{2^2} \frac{2.25/1}{(1+0.0225/1)^{5+2}} + \frac{6(6+1)}{2^2} \frac{102.25}{(1+0.0225/1)^{6+2}}\right]$$

$$= 9.3302$$

c) Is the convexity different in the two cases? Why?

Yes, the convexity for the semiannual bond is smaller. We spread the bond payments out over more periods, which makes the bond's duration slightly less susceptible to interest rate changes.

# Chapter 8

## Swaps

### Question 8.2

a) We first solve for the present value of the cost per three barrels, based on the forward prices:

$$\frac{\$20}{1.06} + \frac{\$21}{(1.065)^2} + \frac{\$22}{(1.07)^3} = 55.3413.$$

We then obtain the swap price per barrel by solving:

$$\frac{x}{1.06} + \frac{x}{(1.065)^2} + \frac{x}{(1.07)^3} = 55.341$$

$$\Leftrightarrow \qquad\qquad x = 20.9519$$

b) We first solve for the present value of the cost per two barrels (Year 2 and Year 3):

$$\frac{\$21}{(1.065)^2} + \frac{\$22}{(1.07)^3} = 36.473.$$

We then obtain the swap price per barrel by solving:

$$\frac{x}{(1.065)^2} + \frac{x}{(1.07)^3} = 36.473$$

$$\Leftrightarrow x \qquad\qquad = 21.481$$

### Question 8.4

The fair swap rate was determined to be $20.952. Therefore, compared to the forward curve price of $20 in one year, we are overpaying $0.952. In Year 2, this overpayment has increased to $0.952 × 1.070024 = 1.01866, where we used the appropriate forward rate to calculate the interest payment. In Year 2, we underpay by $0.048, so that our total cumulative underpayment is $0.97066. In Year 3, this overpayment has increased again to $0.97066 × 1.08007 = 1.048. However, in Year 3, we receive a fixed payment of 20.952, which underpays relative to the forward curve price of $22 by $22 − $20.952 = 1.048. Therefore, our cumulative balance is indeed zero, which was to be shown.

## Question 8.6

In order to answer this question, we use equation (8.14) of the main text. We assumed that the interest rates and the corresponding zero-coupon bonds were:

| Quarter | Interest rate | Zero-coupon price |
|---------|---------------|-------------------|
| 1 | 0.0150 | 0.9852 |
| 2 | 0.0302 | 0.9707 |
| 3 | 0.0457 | 0.9563 |
| 4 | 0.0614 | 0.9422 |
| 5 | 0.0773 | 0.9283 |
| 6 | 0.0934 | 0.9145 |
| 7 | 0.1098 | 0.9010 |
| 8 | 0.1265 | 0.8877 |

Using formula 8.14, we obtain the following per barrel swap prices:

four-quarter swap price: $20.8533

eight-quarter swap price: $20.4284

The total costs of prepaid four- and eight-quarter swaps are the present values of the payment obligations. They are:

four-quarter prepaid swap price: $80.3768

eight-quarter prepaid swap price: $152.9256

## Question 8.8

We use formula (8.8), and replace the forward interest rate with the forward oil prices. In particular, we calculate:

$$X = \frac{\sum_{i=3}^{6} P_0(0,t_i) F_{0,t_i}}{\sum_{i=3}^{6} P_0(0,t_i)} = \$20.3807$$

Therefore, the swap price of a four-quarter oil swap with the first settlement occurring in the third quarter is $20.3807.

## Question 8.10

We use equation (8.6) of the main text to answer this question:

$$X = \frac{\sum_{i=1}^{8} Q_{t_i} P_0(0,t_i) F_{0,t_i}}{\sum_{i=1}^{8} Q_{t_i} P_0(0,t_i)}, \text{ where } Q = [1, 2, 1, 2, 1, 2, 1, 2]$$

After plugging in the relevant variables given in the exercise, we obtain a value of $20.4099 for the swap price.

## Question 8.12

With a swap price of $2.2044, and the forward prices of question 8.11, we can calculate the implied loan amount. We can calculate the net position by subtracting the swap price from the forward prices. The one-quarter implied forward rate is calculated from the zero-coupon bond prices. The column implicit loan balance adds the net position each quarter and the implicit loan balance plus interest of the previous quarter. Please note that the shape of the forward curve—we are initially loaning money, because the swap price is lower than the forward price.

| Quarter | Forward price | Net balance | Forward interest rate | Implicit loan balance |
|---------|---------------|-------------|-----------------------|-----------------------|
| 1 | 2.25 | 0.0456 | 1.0150 | 0.0456 |
| 2 | 2.60 | 0.3955 | 1.0156 | 0.4418 |
| 3 | 2.20 | −0.0042 | 1.0162 | 0.4447 |
| 4 | 1.90 | −0.3046 | 1.0168 | 0.1476 |
| 5 | 2.20 | −0.0043 | 1.0170 | 0.1458 |
| 6 | 2.50 | 0.2954 | 1.0172 | 0.4437 |
| 7 | 2.15 | −0.0543 | 1.0175 | 0.3971 |
| 8 | 1.80 | −0.4042 | 1.0178 | 0.0000 |

## Question 8.14

From the given zero-coupon bond prices, we can calculate the one-quarter forward interest rates. They are:

| Quarter | Forward interest rate |
|---------|----------------------|
| 1 | 1.0150 |
| 2 | 1.0156 |
| 3 | 1.0162 |
| 4 | 1.0168 |
| 5 | 1.0170 |
| 6 | 1.0172 |
| 7 | 1.0175 |
| 8 | 1.0178 |

Now, we can calculate the swap prices for four and eight quarters according to the formula:

$$X = \frac{\sum_{i=1}^{n} P_0(0,t_i) r_0\left(t_{i-1}, t_i\right)}{\sum_{i=1}^{n} P_0(0,t_i)}, \text{ where } n = 4 \text{ or } 8$$

This yields the following prices:

four-quarter fixed swap price: 1.59015 percent

eight-quarter fixed swap price: 1.66096 percent

## Question 8.16

The dollar zero-coupon bond prices for the three years are:

$$P_{0,1} = \frac{1}{1.06} = 0.9434$$

$$P_{0,2} = \frac{1}{(1.06)^2} = 0.8900$$

$$P_{0,3} = \frac{1}{(1.06)^3} = 0.8396$$

$R_*$ is 0.035, the Euro-bond coupon rate. The current exchange rate is 0.9\$/E. Plugging all the above variables into formula (8.13) indeed yields 0.06, the dollar coupon rate:

$$R = \frac{\sum_{i=1}^{3} P_0(0,t_i)R^* F_{0,t_i}/x_0 + P_{0,3}\left(F_{0,t_n}/x_0 - 1\right)}{\sum_{i=1}^{3} P_0(0,t_i)} = \frac{0.098055 + 0.062317}{2.673} = 0.060$$

## Question 8.18

We can use equation (8.13), but there is a complication: We do not have the current spot exchange rate. However, it is possible to back it out by using the methodology of the previous chapters: We know that the following relation must hold:

$$F_{0,1} = X_0 e^{(r-r*)},$$ where the interest rates are already on a quarterly level.

We can back out the interest rates from the given zero-coupon prices. Doing so yields a current exchange rate of 0.90 \$/Euro. $R*$ is the eight-quarter fixed swap price payment of 0.0094572.

By plugging in all the relevant variables into equation 8.13, we can indeed see that this yields a swap rate of 1.66 percent, which is the same rate that we calculated in exercise 8.14.

# Chapter 9

## Parity and Other Option Relationships

### Question 9.2

This problem requires the application of put-call-parity. We have:

$$S_0 - C\,(30, 0.5) + P\,(30, 0.5) - e^{-rT}\,30 = PV\,(dividends)$$

$$\Leftrightarrow \quad PV\,(dividends) = 32 - 4.29 + 2.64 - 29.406 = \$0.944.$$

### Question 9.4

We can make use of the put-call-parity for currency options:

$$+P\,(K, T) = -e^{-r_f T} x_0 + C\,(K, T) + e^{-rT} K$$

$$\Leftrightarrow P\,(K, T) = -e^{-0.04} 0.95 + 0.0571 + e^{-0.06} 0.93 = -0.91275 + 0.0571 + 0.87584 = 0.0202.$$

A \$0.93 strike European put option has a value of \$0.0202.

### Question 9.6

a) We can use put-call-parity to determine the forward price:

$$+ C\,(K, T) - P\,(K, T) = PV\,(forward\,price) - PV\,(strike) = e^{-rT} F_{0,T} - Ke^{-rT}$$

$$\Leftrightarrow F_{0,T} = e^{rT} + C\,(K, T) - P\,(K, T) + Ke^{-rT}$$

$$= e^{0.05*0.5}\,[\$0.0404 - \$0.0141 + \$0.9e^{-0.05*0.5}]$$

$$\Leftrightarrow F_{0,T} = \$0.92697.$$

b) Given the forward price from above and the pricing formula for the forward price, we can find the current spot rate:

$$F_{0,T} = x_0 e^{(r - r_f)T}$$

$$\Leftrightarrow x_0 = F_{0,T}\,e^{-(r - r_f)T} = \$0.92697 e^{-(0.05 - 0.035)0.5} = \$0.92.$$

# Question 9.8

Both equations (9.15) and (9.16) are violated. We use a call bull spread and a put bear spread to profit from these arbitrage opportunities.

| Transaction | $t = 0$ | $S_T < 50$ | $50 \leq S_T \leq 55$ | $S_T > 55$ |
|---|---|---|---|---|
| | | | Expiration or Exercise | |
| Buy 50 strike call | −9 | 0 | $S_T - 50$ | $S_T - 50$ |
| Sell 55 strike call | +10 | 0 | 0 | $55 - S_T$ |
| TOTAL | +1 | 0 | $S_T - 50 > 0$ | $5 > 0$ |

| Transaction | $t = 0$ | $S_T < 50$ | $50 \leq S_T \leq 55$ | $S_T > 55$ |
|---|---|---|---|---|
| | | | Expiration or Exercise | |
| Buy 55 strike put | −6 | $55 - S_T$ | $55 - S_T$ | 0 |
| Sell 50 strike put | 7 | $S_T - 50$ | 0 | 0 |
| TOTAL | +1 | $5 > 0$ | $55 - S_T > 0$ | 0 |

Please note that we initially receive money and that at expiration the profit is nonnegative. We have found arbitrage opportunities.

# Question 9.10

Both equations (9.19) and (9.20) of the textbook are violated. To see this, let us calculate the values. We have:

$$\frac{C(K_1) - C(K_2)}{K_2 - K_1} = \frac{18 - 14}{55 - 50} = 0.8 \text{ and } \frac{C(K_2) - C(K_3)}{K_3 - K_2} = \frac{14 - 9.50}{60 - 55} = 0.9,$$

which violates equation (9.19) and

$$\frac{P(K_2) - P(K_1)}{K_2 - K_1} = \frac{10.75 - 7}{55 - 50} = 0.75 \text{ and } \frac{P(K_3) - P(K_2)}{K_3 - K_2} = \frac{14.45 - 10.75}{60 - 55} = 0.74,$$

which violates equation (9.20).

We calculate lambda in order to know how many options to buy and sell when we construct the butterfly spread that exploits this form of mispricing. Because the strike prices are symmetric around 55, lambda is equal to 0.5.

Therefore, we use a call and put butterfly spread to profit from these arbitrage opportunities.

| Transaction | $t = 0$ | $S_T < 50$ | $50 \leq S_T \leq 55$ | $55 \leq S_T \leq 60$ | $S_T > 60$ |
|---|---|---|---|---|---|
| Buy one 50 strike call | −18 | 0 | $S_T - 50$ | $S_T - 50$ | $S_T - 50$ |
| Sell two 55 strike calls | +28 | 0 | 0 | $110 - 2 \times S_T$ | $110 - 2 \times S_T$ |
| Buy one 60 strike call | −9.50 | 0 | 0 | 0 | $S_T - 60$ |
| TOTAL | +0.50 | 0 | $S_T - 50 \geq 0$ | $60 - S_T \geq 0$ | 0 |

| Transaction | $t = 0$ | $S_T < 50$ | $50 \leq S_T \leq 55$ | $55 \leq S_T \leq 60$ | $S_T > 60$ |
|---|---|---|---|---|---|
| Buy one 50 strike put | −7 | $50 - S_T$ | 0 | 0 | 0 |
| Sell two 55 strike puts | 21.50 | $2 \times S_T - 110$ | $2 \times S_T - 110$ | 0 | 0 |
| Buy one 60 strike put | −14.45 | $60 - S_T$ | $60 - S_T$ | $60 - S_T$ | 0 |
| TOTAL | +0.05 | 0 | $S_T - 50 \geq 0$ | $60 - S_T \geq 0$ | 0 |

Please note that we initially receive money and have nonnegative future payoffs. Therefore, we have found an arbitrage possibility, independent of the prevailing interest rate.

## Question 9.12

a) Equation (9.17) of the textbook is violated. We use a call bear spread to profit from this arbitrage opportunity.

| | | | Expiration or Exercise | |
|---|---|---|---|---|
| Transaction | $t = 0$ | $S_T < 90$ | $90 \leq S_T \leq 95$ | $S_T > 95$ |
| Sell 90 strike call | +10 | 0 | $90 - S_T$ | $90 - S_T$ |
| Buy 95 strike call | −4 | 0 | 0 | $S_T - 95$ |
| TOTAL | +6 | 0 | $90 - S_T > -5$ | −5 |

Please note that we initially receive more money than our biggest possible exposure in the future. Therefore, we have found an arbitrage possibility, independent of the prevailing interest rate.

b) Now, equation (9.17) is not violated anymore. However, we can still construct an arbitrage opportunity, given the information in the exercise. We continue to sell the 90-strike call and buy the 95-strike call, and we loan our initial positive net balance for two years until expiration. It is important that the options be European, because otherwise we would not be able to tell whether the 90-strike call could be exercised against us sometime (note that we do not have information regarding any dividends).

We have the following arbitrage table:

|  |  | Expiration $t = T$ | | |
| --- | --- | --- | --- | --- |
| Transaction | $t = 0$ | $S_T < 90$ | $90 \leq S_T \leq 95$ | $S_T > 95$ |
| Sell 90 strike call | +10 | 0 | $90 - S_T$ | $90 - S_T$ |
| Buy 95 strike call | −5.25 | 0 | 0 | $S_T - 95$ |
| Loan 4.75 | −4.75 | 5.80 | 5.80 | 5.8 |
| TOTAL | 0 | 5.80 | $95.8 - S_T > 0$ | +0.8 |

In all possible future states, we have a strictly positive payoff. We have created something out of nothing—we demonstrated arbitrage.

c)   We will first verify that equation (9.19) is violated. We have:

$$\frac{C(K_1) - C(K_2)}{K_2 - K_1} = \frac{15 - 10}{100 - 90} = 0.5 \text{ and } \frac{C(K_2) - C(K_3)}{K_3 - K_2} = \frac{10 - 6}{105 - 100} = 0.8,$$

which violates equation (9.19).

We calculate lambda in order to know how many options to buy and sell when we construct the butterfly spread that exploits this form of mispricing. Using formula (9.21), we can calculate that lambda is equal to 1/3. To buy and sell round lots, we multiply all the option trades by 3.

We use an asymmetric call and put butterfly spread to profit from these arbitrage opportunities.

| Transaction | $t = 0$ | $S_T < 90$ | $90 \leq S_T \leq 100$ | $100 \leq S_T \leq 105$ | $S_T > 105$ |
| --- | --- | --- | --- | --- | --- |
| Buy one 90 strike calls | −15 | 0 | $S_T - 90$ | $S_T - 90$ | $S_T - 90$ |
| Sell three 100 strike calls | +30 | 0 | 0 | $300 - 3 \times S_T$ | $300 - 3 \times S_T$ |
| Buy two 105 strike calls | −12 | 0 | 0 | 0 | $2 \times S_T - 210$ |
| TOTAL | +3 | 0 | $S_T - 90 \geq 0$ | $210 - 2 \times S_T \geq 0$ | 0 |

We indeed have an arbitrage opportunity.

## Question 9.14

This question is closely related to question 9.13. In this exercise, the strike is not cash anymore but rather one share of Apple. In parts (a) and (b), there is no benefit in keeping Apple longer because the dividend is zero.

a) The underlying asset is the stock of Apple, which does not pay a dividend. Therefore, we have an American call option on a non-dividend-paying stock. It is never optimal to early exercise such an option.

b) The underlying asset is the stock of Apple, and the strike consists of AOL. As AOL does not pay a dividend, the interest rate on AOL is zero. We will therefore never early exercise the put option because we cannot receive earlier any benefits associated with holding Apple— there are none. If Apple is bankrupt, there is no loss from not early exercising because the option is worth max[0, AOL – 0], which is equivalent to one share of AOL because of the limited liability of stock. As AOL does not pay dividends, we are indifferent between holding the option and the stock.

c) For the American call option, dividends on the stock are the reason why we want to receive the stock earlier, and now Apple pays a dividend. We usually benefit from waiting because we can continue to earn interest on the strike. However, in this case, the dividend on AOL remains zero, so we do not have this benefit associated with waiting to exercise. Finally, we saw that there is a second benefit to waiting: the insurance protection, which will not be affected by the zero AOL dividend. Therefore, there now may be circumstances in which we will early exercise, but we will not always early exercise.

For the American put option, no cost is associated with waiting to exercise the option because exercising gives us a share of AOL, which does not pay interest in form of a dividend. However, by early exercising we will forgo the interest we could earn on Apple. Therefore, it is again never optimal to exercise the American put option early.

## Question 9.16

Short call perspective:

| Transaction | $t = 0$ | time = $T$ $S_T \leq K$ | time = $T$ $S_T > K$ |
|---|---|---|---|
| Sell call | $+C^B$ | 0 | $K - S_T$ |
| Buy put | $-P^A$ | $K - S_T$ | 0 |
| Buy share | $-S^A$ | $S_T$ | $S_T$ |
| Borrow @ $r_B$ | $+Ke^{-r_BT}$ | $-K$ | $-K$ |
| TOTAL | $C^B - P^A - S^A + Ke^{-r_BT}$ | 0 | 0 |

In order to preclude arbitrage, we must have: $C^B - P^A - S^A + Ke^{-r_BT} \leq 0$.

Long call perspective:

| Transaction | $t = 0$ | time = $T$ $S_T \leq K$ | time = $T$ $S_T > K$ |
|---|---|---|---|
| Buy call | $-C^A$ | 0 | $S_T - K$ |
| Sell put | $+P^B$ | $S_T - K$ | 0 |
| Sell share | $+S^B$ | $-S_T$ | $-S_T$ |
| Lend @ $r_L$ | $-Ke^{-r_L T}$ | $+K$ | $+K$ |
| TOTAL | $-C^A + P^B + S^B - Ke^{-r_L T}$ | 0 | 0 |

In order to preclude arbitrage, we must have: $-C^A + P^B + S^B - Ke^{-r_L T} \leq 0$.

## Question 9.18.

a) Since the strike prices are symmetric, lambda is equal to 0.5. Therefore, to buy a long butterfly spread, we buy the 165-strike call, sell two 170 strike calls and buy one 175 strike call.

$$\frac{C(K_1) - C(K_2)}{K_2 - K_1} = \frac{6.25 - 3.20}{170 - 165} = 0.61 \quad and \quad \frac{C(K_2) - C(K_3)}{K_3 - K_2} = \frac{3.20 - 1.43}{175 - 170} = 0.354$$

Convexity holds.

b)

$$\frac{C(K_1) - C(K_2)}{K_2 - K_1} = \frac{6.15 - 3.30}{170 - 165} = 0.57 \quad and \quad \frac{C(K_2) - C(K_3)}{K_3 - K_2} = \frac{3.30 - 1.38}{175 - 165} = 0.384$$

Convexity holds.

c) A market maker can buy a butterfly spread at the prices we sell it for. Therefore, the above convexity conditions are the ones relevant for market makers. Convexity is not violated from a market maker's perspective.

# Chapter 10

## Binomial Option Pricing: Basic Concepts

### Question 10.2

a) Using the formulas of the textbook, we obtain the following results:

$$\Delta = 0.7$$
$$B = -53.8042$$
$$price = 16.1958$$

b) If we observe a price of $17, then the option price is too high relative to its theoretical value. We sell the option and synthetically create a call option for $19.196. In order to do so, we buy 0.7 units of the share and borrow $53.804. These transactions yield no risk and a profit of $0.804.

c) If we observe a price of $15.50, then the option price is too low relative to its theoretical value. We buy the option and synthetically create a short position in an option. In order to do so, we sell 0.7 units of the share and lend $53.8042. These transactions yield no risk and a profit of $0.696.

### Question 10.4

I downloaded weekly price data from finance.yahoo.com for Microsoft, from January 3, 2007 to December 27, 2011. To do so, go to finance.yahoo.com, enter a ticker symbol, go to historical prices, and then specify a timeframe and frequency. Scroll to the bottom of the page and download data to spreadsheet. Once you open the spreadsheet, discard all other prices except for adjusted close. This price takes into account dividend payments and stock splits and is appropriate to calculate returns. Before you calculate returns, note that Yahoo! orders prices with the most recent first, so we have to sort prices by date. Then, calculate returns as $\ln(P(t)/P(t-1))$, and calculate the standard deviation of prices using the stdev.s (Excel 2010) function. The results are as follows:

a) Using all data, the weekly standard deviation is 0.0405. We annualize this standard deviation by multiplying it with the square root of 52 to get 0.29227

| MSFT, weekly | 2007 | 2008 | 2009 | 2010 | 2011 |
|---|---|---|---|---|---|
| StDev | 0.034 | 0.053 | 0.047 | 0.032 | 0.030 |
| StDev * Sqrt(52) | 0.244 | 0.384 | 0.342 | 0.232 | 0.217 |

b) We can see from the table that standard deviation varies considerably by year. During the financial crisis of 2008, the standard deviation was highest.

| MSFT, weekly | 2007, 1st | 2007, 2nd | 2008, 1st | 2008, 2nd | 2009, 1st | 2009, 2nd | 2010, 1st | 2010, 2nd | 2011, 1st | 2011, 2nd |
|---|---|---|---|---|---|---|---|---|---|---|
| StDev | 0.022 | 0.042 | 0.037 | 0.066 | 0.062 | 0.027 | 0.034 | 0.028 | 0.024 | 0.036 |
| StDev * Sqrt(52) | 0.159 | 0.304 | 0.268 | 0.478 | 0.447 | 0.196 | 0.246 | 0.202 | 0.170 | 0.258 |

c) We see that standard deviation varies substantially between the first and second half of the year. We can see again the effect of the financial crisis, with very high standard deviations in 2008, second half and 2009, first half. This exercise suggests that it is not easy to calculate standard deviations, and that we have to think about the appropriate time frame over which we estimate it.

## Question 10.6

The stock prices evolve according to the following picture:

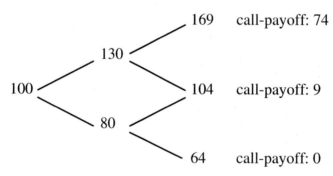

Since we have two binomial steps, and a time to expiration of one year, $h$ is equal to 0.5. Therefore, we can calculate with the usual formulas for the respective nodes:

| $t = 0, S = 100$ | $t = 1, S = 80$ | $t = 1, S = 130$ |
|---|---|---|
| $\Delta = 0.691$ | $\Delta = 0.225$ | $\Delta = 1$ |
| $B = -49.127$ | $B = -13.835$ | $B = -91.275$ |
| $price = 19.994$ | $price = 4.165$ | $price = 38.725$ |

## Question 10.8

The stock prices evolve according to the following picture:

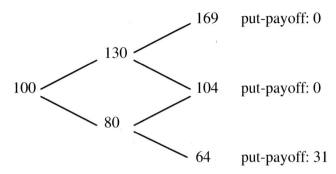

Since we have two binomial steps, and a time to expiration of one year, $h$ is equal to 0.5. Therefore, we can calculate with the usual formulas for the respective nodes:

| $t = 0, S = 100$ | $t = 1, S = 80$ | $t = 1, S = 130$ |
|---|---|---|
| $\Delta = -0.3088$ | $\Delta = -0.775$ | $\Delta = 0$ |
| $B = 38.569$ | $B = 77.4396$ | $B = 0$ |
| $price = 7.6897$ | $price = 15.4396$ | $price = 0$ |

## Question 10.10

We must compare the results of the equivalent European put that we calculated in exercise 10.6. with the value of immediate exercise. In 10.6., we calculated:

| $t = 1, S = 80$ | $t = 1, S = 130$ |
|---|---|
| $\Delta = -0.775$ | $\Delta = 0$ |
| $B = 77.4396$ | $B = 0$ |
| $price = 15.4396$ | $price = 0$ |
| immediate exercise = | immediate exercise |
| max $(95 - 80, 0) = 15$ | $= \max(95 - 130, 0) = 0$ |

Since the value of immediate exercise is smaller than or equal to the continuation value (of the European options) at both nodes of the tree, there is no benefit to exercising the options before expiration. Therefore, we use the European option values when calculating the $t = 0$ option price:

$t = 0, S = 100$

$\Delta = -0.3088$

$B = 38.569$

*price* $= 7.6897$

immediate exercise $= \max(95 - 100, 0) = 0$

Since the option price is again higher than the value of immediate exercise (which is zero), there is no benefit to exercising the option at $t = 0$. Since it is never optimal to exercise earlier, the early exercise option has no value. The value of the American put option is identical to the value of the European put option.

## Question 10.12

a) We can calculate for the different nodes of the tree:

|  | node uu | node ud = du | node dd |
|---|---|---|---|
| delta | 1 | 0.8966 | 0 |
| B | −92.5001 | −79.532 | 0 |
| call premium | 56.6441 | 15.0403 | 0 |
| value of early exercise | 54.1442 | 10.478 | 0 |

Using these values at the previous node and at the initial node yields:

|  | $t = 0$ | node $d$ | node $u$ |
|---|---|---|---|
| delta | 0.7400 | 0.4870 | 0.9528 |
| B | −55.7190 | −35.3748 | −83.2073 |
| call premium | 18.2826 | 6.6897 | 33.1493 |
| value of early exercise | 5 | 0 | 27.1250 |

Please note that in all instances the value of immediate exercise is smaller than the continuation value, the (European) call premium. Therefore, the value of the European call and the American call are identical.

b) We can calculate similarly the binomial prices at each node in the tree. We can calculate for the different nodes of the tree:

|  | node *uu* | node *ud* = *du* | node *dd* |
|---|---|---|---|
| delta | 0 | −0.1034 | −1 |
| *B* | 0 | 12.968 | 92.5001 |
| put premium | 0 | 2.0624 | 17.904 |
| value of early exercise | 0 | 0 | 20.404 |

Using these values at the previous node and at the initial node yields:

|  | *t* = 0 | node *d* | node *u* |
|---|---|---|---|
| delta | −0.26 | −0.513 | −0.047 |
| *B* | 31.977 | 54.691 | 6.859 |
| put premium | 5.979 | 10.387 | 1.091 |
| value of early exercise | 0 | 8.6307 | 0 |

c) From the previous tables, we can see that at the node dd, it is optimal to early exercise the American put option because the value of early exercise exceeds the continuation value. Therefore, we must use the value of 20.404 in all relevant previous nodes when we back out the prices of the American put option. We have for nodes *d* and 0 (the other nodes remain unchanged):

|  | *t* = 0 | node *d* |
|---|---|---|
| delta | −0.297 | −0.594 |
| *B* | 36.374 | 63.005 |
| put premium | 6.678 | 11.709 |
| value of early exercise | 0 | 8.6307 |

The price of the American put option is indeed 6.678.

## Question 10.14

a) We can calculate *u* and *d* as follows:

$$u = e^{(r-\delta)h+\sigma\sqrt{h}} = e^{(0.08)\times0.25+0.3\times\sqrt{0.25}} = 1.1853$$

$$d = e^{(r-\delta)h+\sigma\sqrt{h}} = e^{(0.08)\times0.25+0.3\times\sqrt{0.25}} = 0.8781$$

b) We need to calculate the values at the relevant nodes in order to price the European call option:

| | $t = 0$ | node $d$ | node $u$ |
|---|---|---|---|
| delta | 0.6074 | 0.1513 | 1 |
| $B$ | −20.187 | −4.5736 | −39.208 |
| call premium | 4.110 | 0.7402 | 8.204 |

c) We can calculate at the relevant nodes (or, equivalently, you can use put-call-parity for the European put option):

| European put | $t = 0$ | node $d$ | node $u$ |
|---|---|---|---|
| delta | −0.3926 | −0.8487 | 0 |
| $B$ | 18.245 | 34.634 | 0 |
| put premium | 2.5414 | 4.8243 | 0 |

For the American put option, we have to compare the premia at each node with the value of early exercise. We see from the following table that at the node $d$, it is advantageous to exercise the option early; consequently, we use the value of early exercise when we calculate the value of the put option.

| American put | $t = 0$ | node $d$ | node $u$ |
|---|---|---|---|
| delta | −0.3968 | −0.8487 | 0 |
| $B$ | 18.441 | 34.634 | 0 |
| put premium | 2.5687 | 4.8243 | 0 |
| value of early exercise | 0 | 4.8762 | 0 |

## Question 10.16

a) We can calculate the price of the call currency option in a very similar way to our previous calculations. We simply replace the dividend yield with the foreign interest rate in our formulas. Thus, we have:

| | node $uu$ | node $ud = du$ | node $dd$ |
|---|---|---|---|
| delta | 0.9925 | 0.9925 | 0.1964 |
| $B$ | −0.8415 | −0.8415 | −0.1314 |
| call premium | 0.4734 | 0.1446 | 0.0150 |

Using these call premia at all previous nodes yields:

|  | $t = 0$ | node $d$ | node $u$ |
|---|---|---|---|
| delta | 0.7038 | 0.5181 | 0.9851 |
| B | −0.5232 | 0.1243 | −0.3703 |
| call premium | 0.0587 | −0.8332 | 0.2544 |

The price of the European call option is $0.1243.

b) For the American call option, the binomial approach yields:

|  | node $uu$ | node $ud = du$ | node $dd$ |
|---|---|---|---|
| delta | 0.9925 | 0.9925 | 0.1964 |
| B | −0.8415 | −0.8415 | −0.1314 |
| call premium | 0.4734 | 0.1446 | 0.0150 |
| value of early exercise | 0.4748 | 0.1436 | 0 |

Using the maximum of the call premium and the value of early exercise at the previous nodes and at the initial node yields:

|  | $t = 0$ | node $d$ | node $u$ |
|---|---|---|---|
| delta | 0.7056 | 0.5181 | 0.9894 |
| B | −0.5247 | −0.3703 | −0.8374 |
| call premium | 0.1245 | 0.0587 | 0.2549 |
| value of early exercise | 0.07 | 0 | 0.2540 |

The price of the American call option is: $0.1245.

## Question 10.18

aa) We now have to inverse the interest rates: We have a yen-denominated option, therefore, the dollar interest rate becomes the foreign interest rate. With these changes, and equipped with an exchange rate of Y120/$ and a strike of Y120, we can proceed with our standard binomial procedure.

|  | node $uu$ | node $ud = du$ | node $dd$ |
|---|---|---|---|
| delta | 0.9835 | 0.1585 | 0 |
| B | −119.6007 | −17.4839 | 0 |
| call premium | 9.3756 | 1.0391 | 0 |

Using these call premia at all previous nodes yields:

|  | $t = 0$ | node $d$ | node $u$ |
|---|---|---|---|
| delta | 0.3283 | 0.0802 | 0.5733 |
| $B$ | −36.6885 | −8.4614 | −66.8456 |
| call premium. | 2.7116 | 0.5029 | 5.0702 |

The price of the European yen-denominated call option is $2.7116.

ab) For the American call option, the binomial approach yields:

|  | node $uu$ | node $ud = du$ | node $dd$ |
|---|---|---|---|
| delta | 0.9835 | 0.1585 | 0 |
| $B$ | −119.6007 | −17.4839 | 0 |
| call premium | 9.3756 | 1.0391 | 0 |
| value of early exercise | 11.1439 | 0 | 0 |

Using the maximum of the call premium and the value of early exercise at the previous nodes and at the initial node yields:

|  | $t = 0$ | node $d$ | node $u$ |
|---|---|---|---|
| delta | 0.3899 | 0.0802 | 0.6949 |
| $B$ | −43.6568 | −8.4614 | −81.2441 |
| call premium | 3.1257 | 0.5029 | 5.9259 |
| value of early exercise | 0 | 0 | 5.4483 |

b) For the yen-denominated put option, we have:

|  | node $uu$ | node $ud = du$ | node $dd$ |
|---|---|---|---|
| delta | 0 | −0.8249 | −0.9835 |
| $B$ | 0 | 102.1168 | 119.6007 |
| put premium | 0 | 5.7287 | 17.2210 |
| value of early exercise | 0 | 3.1577 | 15.8997 |

We can clearly see that early exercise is never optimal at those stages. We can therefore calculate at the previous nodes:

| | $t = 0$ | node $d$ | node $u$ |
|---|---|---|---|
| delta | −0.6229 | −0.8870 | −0.3939 |
| $B$ | 82.1175 | 110.7413 | 52.3571 |
| put premium | 7.37 | 11.602 | 2.9372 |
| value of early exercise | 0 | 8.2322 | 0 |

We can see that the American and the European put option must have the same price, since it is never optimal to exercise the American put option early. The price of the put option is 7.37.

c) The benefit of early exercise for a put option is to receive the strike price earlier on and start earning interest on it. The cost associated with early exercising a put is to stop earning income on the asset we give up. In this case, the strike is 120 yen, and the yen interest rate is not very favorable compared to the dollar interest rate. We would give up a high yield instrument and receive a low yield instrument when we early exercise the put option. This is not beneficial, and it is reflected by the nonoptimality of early exercise of the put option.

For the call option, the opposite is true: When exercising the call option, we receive a dollar and give up 120 yen. Therefore, we receive the high-yield instrument, and if the exchange rate moves in our favor, we want to exercise the option before expiration.

## Question 10.20

a) We have to use the formulas of the textbook to calculate the stock tree and the prices of the options. Remember that while it is possible to calculate a delta, the option price is just the value of B because it does not cost anything to enter into a futures contract. In particular, this yields the following prices: For the European call and put, we have: *premium* = 122.9537. The prices must be equal due to put-call-parity.

b) We can calculate for the American call option: *premium* = 124.3347 and for the American put option: *premium* = 124.3347.

c) We have the following time 0 replicating portfolios:

For the European call option:

> Buy 0.5371 futures contracts.
>
> Borrow 122.9537

For the European put option:

> Sell 0.4141 futures contracts.
>
> Borrow 122.9537

## Question 10.22

a) The price of an American call option with a strike of 95 is $24.1650.

b) The price of an American put option with a strike of 95 is $15.2593.

c) Now, for the American 100-strike call option we have a premium of $15.2593 and for the European put option a premium of $24.165. Both option prices increase as we would have expected, and the relation we observed in question 10.19 continues to hold.

# Chapter 11

## Binomial Option Pricing: Selected Topics

### Question 11.2

By introducing a nonzero interest rate, we increase the cost of early exercise because we pay the strike before expiration and lose interest on it. We see that we only exercise the call with a strike of 70. The value of the European 70-strike call is $27.69; the value of immediate exercise is $30.

The decisive condition, derived from put-call-parity, is now:

$$C = Se^{-\delta} - Ke^{-r} + P = 100 \times 0.92311 - K \times 0.92311 + P = 92.31164 - 0.92311K + P$$

Therefore, we will exercise whenever

$$100 - K > 92.31164 - 0.92311K + P$$

$$\Leftrightarrow P < 7.688 - 0.07688K$$

This condition is indeed fulfilled at a strike price of 70. Clearly, this boundary is attained earlier than the boundary of exercise 11.1, so we will stop early exercise at lower strike prices when the interest rates are high.

### Question 11.4

a) Early exercise occurs only at a strike price of 130. The value of the one period binomial European 130 strike put is $26.38, while the value of immediate exercise is $130 - 100 = 30$.

b) From put-call-parity, we observe the following:

$$P = Ke^{-r} - Se^{-\delta} + C = K \times 0.9231164 - S + C = 92.31164K - S + C$$

Clearly, as long as $K - 100$ is larger than $92.31164K - 100 + C$ or $C < 0.07688K$, we will exercise the option early. Already at a strike of 120, $0.07688 \times 120 = 9.2256$ is smaller than the value of the European call option with a strike of 120 (with a price of $10.30), which means that we do not exercise prior to expiration.

c) The value of a call falls when the strike price increases. From part (b), we learned that the decisive criterion was that $C < 0.07688K$. Therefore, if this criterion is fulfilled for some threshold $K(*)$, it is fulfilled for every $K$ above $K(*)$.

## Question 11.6

We now have from put-call-parity:

$$P = Ke^{-r} - Se^{-\delta} + C = K - S \times 0.92311 + C = 0.92311K - 92.31164 + C$$

We would exercise early if:

$$K - 100 > K - 92.31164 + C$$

$$\Leftrightarrow C < -7.688,$$

which can never be true. It is never optimal to early exercise because the sole advantage of early exercise, receiving the interest on the strike earlier, has been removed.

## Question 11.8

For the following questions, we will report the first two of the 10 nodes. We have for the European call options of strike 70, 80, 90 and 100:

Delta and B:

| | K = 70 | | K = 80 | | K = 90 | | K = 100 |
|---|---|---|---|---|---|---|---|
| | 0.98 | | 0.94 | | 0.88 | | 0.77 |
| | −62.84 | | −66.81 | | −68.35 | | −63.16 |
| 0.95 | | 0.88 | | 0.79 | | 0.66 | |
| −58.76 | | −59.44 | | −57.40 | | −50.19 | |
| | 0.91 | | 0.81 | | 0.68 | | 0.54 |
| | −55.96 | | −53.66 | | −48.32 | | −39.16 |

Call option price and gamma, the required rate of return:

| | K = 70 | | K = 80 | | K = 90 | | K = 100 |
|---|---|---|---|---|---|---|---|
| | 110.83 | | 110.83 | | 110.83 | | 110.83 |
| | 45.95 | | 37.38 | | 29.21 | | 22.73 |
| 100.00 | 0.24 | 100.00 | 0.27 | 100.00 | 0.31 | 100.00 | 0.34 |
| 36.14 | | 28.34 | | 21.16 | | 15.96 | |
| 0.26 | 91.68 | 0.30 | 91.68 | 0.34 | 91.68 | 0.376 | 91.68 |
| | 27.77 | | 20.56 | | 14.17 | | 10.06 |
| | 0.29 | | 0.33 | | 0.39 | | 0.42 |

Delta and B:

| | K = 110 | | K = 120 | | K = 130 |
|---|---|---|---|---|---|
| | 0.67 | | 0.55 | | 0.43 |
| | −57.32 | | −48.16 | | −39.00 |
| 0.54 | | 0.43 | | 0.31 | |
| −42.79 | | −34.46 | | −26.13 | |
| | 0.40 | | 0.29 | | 0.19 |
| | −30.24 | | −22.54 | | −14.83 |

Call option price and gamma:

| | K = 110 | | K = 120 | | K = 130 |
|---|---|---|---|---|---|
| | 110.83 | | 110.83 | | 110.83 |
| | 16.63 | | 12.52 | | 8.41 |
| 100.00 | 0.39 | 100.00 | 0.41 | 100.00 | 0.47 |
| 11.14 | | 8.18 | | 5.22 | |
| 0.41 | 91.68 | 0.44 | 91.68 | 0.49 | 91.68 |
| | 6.30 | | 4.36 | | 2.41 |
| | 0.48 | | 0.50 | | 0.57 |

We clearly see that the more the option is out-of-the-money, the higher the required expected return is. This is a consequence of the option becoming more and more leveraged as it moves out of the money.

## Question 11.10

For the following questions, we will, due to space limitations, only report the first two of the ten nodes. We have for the European put options of strike 70, 80, 90 and 100:

Delta and B:

| | K = 70 | | K = 80 | | K = 90 | | K = 100 |
|---|---|---|---|---|---|---|---|
| | −0.02 | | −0.06 | | −0.12 | | −0.23 |
| | 2.29 | | 7.63 | | 15.40 | | 29.89 |
| −0.05 | | −0.12 | | −0.21 | | −0.34 | |
| 5.85 | | 14.41 | | 25.68 | | 42.12 | |
| | −0.09 | | −0.19 | | −0.32 | | −0.46 |
| | 9.18 | | 20.79 | | 35.43 | | 53.90 |

Put option price and gamma, the required rate of return:

| | K = 70 | | K = 80 | | K = 90 | | K = 100 |
|---|---|---|---|---|---|---|---|
| | 110.83 | | 110.83 | | 110.83 | | 110.83 |
| | 0.25 | | 0.99 | | 2.13 | | 4.94 |
| 100.00 | −0.51 | 100.00 | −0.41 | 100.00 | −0.37 | 100.00 | −0.28 |
| 0.75 | | 2.19 | | 4.24 | | 8.27 | |
| −0.41 | 91.68 | −0.32 | 91.68 | −0.28 | 91.68 | −0.21 | 91.68 |
| | 1.23 | | 3.32 | | 6.23 | | 11.43 |
| | −0.39 | | −0.30 | | −0.25 | | −0.18 |

Delta and B:

| | K = 110 | | K = 120 | | K = 130 |
|---|---|---|---|---|---|
| | −0.33 | | −0.45 | | −0.57 |
| | 45.04 | | 63.51 | | 81.97 |
| −0.46 | | −0.57 | | −0.69 | |
| 58.75 | | 76.31 | | 93.87 | |
| | −0.60 | | −0.71 | | −0.81 |
| | 72.12 | | 89.13 | | 106.14 |

Call option price and gamma:

| | K = 110 | | K = 120 | | K = 130 |
|---|---|---|---|---|---|
| | 110.83 | | 110.83 | | 110.83 |
| | 8.16 | | 13.35 | | 18.55 |
| 100.00 | −0.24 | 100.00 | −0.19 | 100.00 | −0.16 |
| 12.68 | | 18.95 | | 25.23 | |
| −0.18 | 91.68 | −0.13 | 91.68 | −0.11 | 91.68 |
| | 16.98 | | 24.34 | | 31.69 |
| | −0.15 | | −0.11 | | −0.09 |

We clearly see that the more the put option is out-of-the-money, the lower the required expected return is.

## Question 11.12

For $n = 3$, $u$ and $d$ are calculated as follows:

$$u = e^{(r-\delta)h + \sigma\sqrt{h}} = e^{(0.08)\times 1/3 + 0.3\times\sqrt{1/3}} = 1.2212$$

$$d = e^{(r-\delta)h - \sigma\sqrt{h}} = e^{(0.08)\times 1/3 - 0.3\times\sqrt{1/3}} = 0.8637$$

Now we can calculate $p^* = \dfrac{e^{(r-\delta)h} - d}{u - d} = 0.4568$

| $n - i$ | Stock price | Probability |
|---|---|---|
| 0 | 182.141786 | 0.09532291 |
| 1 | 128.814742 | 0.34004825 |
| 2 | 91.1006651 | 0.40435476 |
| 3 | 64.4284267 | 0.16027409 |

The figure looks like:

Risk-neutral distribution of 1-year stock prices for n = 3

for $n = 10$, we have:

$$u = e^{(r-\delta)h + \sigma\sqrt{h}} = e^{(0.08)\times 1/10 + 0.3\times\sqrt{1/10}} = 1.1083$$

$$d = e^{(r-\delta)h - \sigma\sqrt{h}} = e^{(0.08)\times 1/10 - 0.3\times\sqrt{1/10}} = 0.9168$$

Now we can calculate $p^* = \dfrac{e^{(r-\delta)h} - d}{u - d} = 0.4763$

| $n - i$ | Stock price | Probability |
|---|---|---|
| 0 | 279.738009 | 0.00060091 |
| 1 | 231.392829 | 0.00660713 |
| 2 | 191.402811 | 0.03269085 |
| 3 | 158.32399 | 0.0958508 |
| 4 | 130.961953 | 0.18443127 |
| 5 | 108.328707 | 0.24334174 |
| 6 | 89.6070076 | 0.22296472 |
| 7 | 74.1208498 | 0.14008734 |
| 8 | 61.3110573 | 0.0577605 |
| 9 | 50.7150924 | 0.014113 |
| 10 | 41.9503547 | 0.00155174 |

The figure looks like:

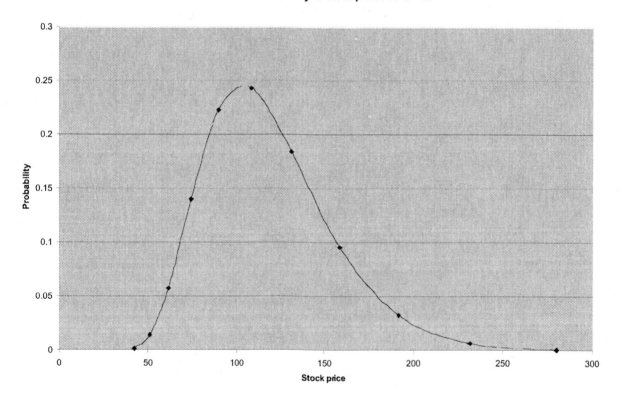

## Question 11.14

a) We can calculate the forward prices as:

$$F_{0,4 \text{ months}} = 100e^{0.08 \times 1/3} = 102.7025$$
$$F_{0,8 \text{ months}} = 100e^{0.08 \times 2/3} = 105.4781$$
$$F_{0,1 \text{ year}} = 100e^{0.08} = 108.3287$$

b) After $t = 1/3$ years, we have:

| Stock price | Probability |
|---|---|
| 122.124611 | 0.45680665 |
| 86.3692561 | 0.54319335 |

This yields an expectation of 102.70254, equivalent to the forward price of part (a). After $t = 2/3$ years, we have:

| Stock price | Probability |
|---|---|
| 149.144206 | 0.20867232 |
| 105.478118 | 0.49626867 |
| 74.596484 | 0.29505901 |

This yields an expectation of 105.4781, equivalent to the forward price of part (a). After one year, we have:

| Stock price | Probability |
|---|---|
| 182.141781 | 0.0953229 |
| 128.814741 | 0.34004825 |
| 91.1006658 | 0.40435476 |
| 64.4284283 | 0.16027409 |

This yields an expectation of 108.3287, equivalent to the forward price of part (a).

# Question 11.16

## Stock Tree

| 0 | 1 | 2 | 3 | 4 | 5 | 6 | 7 | 8 |
|---|---|---|---|---|---|---|---|---|
| | | | | | | | | 233.621 |
| | | | | | | | 210.110 | |
| | | | | | | 188.966 | | 188.966 |
| | | | | | 169.949 | | 169.949 | |
| | | | | 152.847 | | 152.847 | | 152.847 |
| | | | 137.465 | | 137.465 | | 137.465 | |
| | | 123.631 | | 123.631 | | 123.631 | | 123.631 |
| | 111.190 | | 111.190 | | 111.190 | | 111.190 | |
| 100.000 | | 95.000 | | 100.000 | | 100.000 | | 100.000 |
| | 89.937 | | 89.937 | | 89.937 | | 89.937 | |
| | | 80.886 | | 80.886 | | 80.886 | | 80.886 |
| | | | 72.746 | | 72.746 | | 72.746 | |
| | | | | 65.425 | | 65.425 | | 65.425 |
| | | | | | 58.841 | | 58.841 | |
| | | | | | | 52.920 | | 52.920 |
| | | | | | | | 47.594 | |
| | | | | | | | | 42.804 |

## European Call

| 0 | 1 | 2 | 3 | 4 | 5 | 6 | 7 | 8 |
|---|---|---|---|---|---|---|---|---|
| | | | | | | | | 138.621 |
| | | | | | | | 114.746 | |
| | | | | | | 93.500 | | 93.966 |
| | | | | | 74.600 | | 74.836 | |
| | | | | 57.798 | | 57.829 | | 57.847 |
| | | | 43.327 | | 42.719 | | 42.554 | |
| | | 31.432 | | 30.213 | | 28.976 | | 28.631 |
| | 22.118 | | 20.571 | | 18.736 | | 16.442 | |
| 15.140 | | 13.563 | | 11.670 | | 9.221 | | 5.000 |
| | 8.703 | | 7.065 | | 5.080 | | 2.431 | |
| | | 4.183 | | 2.760 | | 1.182 | | 0.000 |
| | | | 1.483 | | 0.575 | | 0.000 | |
| | | | | 0.280 | | 0.000 | | 0.000 |
| | | | | | 0.000 | | 0.000 | |
| | | | | | | 0.000 | | 0.000 |
| | | | | | | | 0.000 | |
| | | | | | | | | 0.000 |

## American Call

| C0 | C1 | C2 | C3 | C4 | C5 | C6 | C7 | C8 |
|---|---|---|---|---|---|---|---|---|
|  |  |  |  |  |  |  |  | 138.621 |
|  |  |  |  |  |  |  | 115.110 |  |
|  |  |  |  |  |  | 93.966 |  | 93.966 |
|  |  |  |  |  | 74.949 |  | 74.949 |  |
|  |  |  |  | 57.981 |  | 57.884 |  | 57.847 |
|  |  |  | 43.422 |  | 42.746 |  | 42.554 |  |
|  |  | 31.482 |  | 30.226 |  | 28.976 |  | 28.631 |
|  | 22.144 |  | 20.578 |  | 18.736 |  | 16.442 |  |
| 15.153 |  | 13.566 |  | 11.670 |  | 9.221 |  | 5.000 |
|  | 8.704 |  | 7.065 |  | 5.080 |  | 2.431 |  |
|  |  | 4.183 |  | 2.760 |  | 1.182 |  | 0.000 |
|  |  |  | 1.483 |  | 0.575 |  | 0.000 |  |
|  |  |  |  | 0.280 |  | 0.000 |  | 0.000 |
|  |  |  |  |  | 0.000 |  | 0.000 |  |
|  |  |  |  |  |  | 0.000 |  | 0.000 |
|  |  |  |  |  |  |  | 0.000 |  |
|  |  |  |  |  |  |  |  | 0.000 |

## European Put

| C0 | C1 | C2 | C3 | C4 | C5 | C6 | C7 | C8 |
|---|---|---|---|---|---|---|---|---|
|  |  |  |  |  |  |  |  | 0.000 |
|  |  |  |  |  |  |  | 0.000 |  |
|  |  |  |  |  |  | 0.000 |  | 0.000 |
|  |  |  |  |  | 0.000 |  | 0.000 |  |
|  |  |  |  | 0.000 |  | 0.000 |  | 0.000 |
|  |  |  | 0.458 |  | 0.000 |  | 0.000 |  |
|  |  | 1.819 |  | 0.909 |  | 0.000 |  | 0.000 |
|  | 4.265 |  | 3.169 |  | 1.804 |  | 0.000 |  |
| 7.713 |  | 6.711 |  | 5.414 |  | 3.582 |  | 0.000 |
|  | 11.194 |  | 10.263 |  | 9.006 |  | 7.110 |  |
|  |  | 15.742 |  | 15.146 |  | 14.420 |  | 14.114 |
|  |  |  | 21.342 |  | 21.373 |  | 21.762 |  |
|  |  |  |  | 27.745 |  | 28.506 |  | 29.575 |
|  |  |  |  |  | 34.444 |  | 35.580 |  |
|  |  |  |  |  |  | 40.857 |  | 42.080 |
|  |  |  |  |  |  |  | 46.757 |  |
|  |  |  |  |  |  |  |  | 52.196 |

American Put

| | | | | | | | | |
|---|---|---|---|---|---|---|---|---|
| | | | | | | | | 0.000 |
| | | | | | | | 0.000 | |
| | | | | | | 0.000 | | 0.000 |
| | | | | | 0.000 | | 0.000 | |
| | | | | 0.000 | | 0.000 | | 0.000 |
| | | | 0.458 | | 0.000 | | 0.000 | |
| | | 1.835 | | 0.909 | | 0.000 | | 0.000 |
| | 4.353 | | 3.201 | | 1.804 | | 0.000 | |
| 7.979 | | 6.870 | | 5.477 | | 3.582 | | 0.000 |
| | 11.637 | | 10.548 | | 9.131 | | 7.110 | |
| | | 16.468 | | 15.651 | | 14.668 | | 14.114 |
| | | | 22.509 | | 22.254 | | 22.254 | |
| | | | | 29.575 | | 29.575 | | 29.575 |
| | | | | | 36.159 | | 36.159 | |
| | | | | | | 42.080 | | 42.080 |
| | | | | | | | 47.406 | |
| | | | | | | | | 52.196 |

## Question 11.18

We will use the methodology introduced by Hull, which is described in the main textbook. We can calculate:

$$u = 1.2005 \qquad S = 50.0000 \qquad K = 45.00$$
$$d = 0.8670 \qquad F = 46.0792 \qquad \text{dividend} = 4.0000$$
$$p = 0.4594 \qquad t = 1.0000 \qquad r = 0.0800$$
$$n = 4.0000 \qquad h = 0.2500 \qquad \text{sigma} = 0.3255$$
$$\text{time to div } 0.2500$$

American Call

|          |          |          |          | 95.7188  |
|----------|----------|----------|----------|----------|
|          |          |          |          | 50.7188  |
|          |          |          | 79.7304  |          |
|          |          |          | 35.6215  |          |
|          |          | 66.4127  |          | 69.1230  |
|          |          | 23.1772  |          | 24.1230  |
|          | 59.3195  |          | 57.5771  |          |
|          | 14.3195  |          | 13.4682  |          |
| 50.0000  |          | 47.9597  |          | 49.9170  |
| 8.4551   |          | 7.2380   |          | 4.9170   |
|          | 43.3480  |          | 41.5791  |          |
|          | 3.7876   |          | 2.2141   |          |
|          |          | 34.6340  |          | 36.0474  |
|          |          | 0.9970   |          | 0.0000   |
|          |          |          | 30.0263  |          |
|          |          |          | 0.0000   |          |
|          |          |          |          | 26.0315  |
|          |          |          |          | 0.0000   |

European Call

|          |          |          |          | 95.7188  |
|----------|----------|----------|----------|----------|
|          |          |          |          | 50.7188  |
|          |          |          | 79.7304  |          |
|          |          |          | 35.6215  |          |
|          |          | 66.4127  |          | 69.1230  |
|          |          | 23.1772  |          | 24.1230  |
|          | 59.3195  |          | 57.5771  |          |
|          | 14.2721  |          | 13.4682  |          |
| 50.0000  |          | 47.9597  |          | 49.9170  |
| 8.4338   |          | 7.2380   |          | 4.9170   |
|          | 43.3480  |          | 41.5791  |          |
|          | 3.7876   |          | 2.2141   |          |
|          |          | 34.6340  |          | 36.0474  |
|          |          | 0.9970   |          | 0.0000   |
|          |          |          | 30.0263  |          |
|          |          |          | 0.0000   |          |
|          |          |          |          | 26.0315  |
|          |          |          |          | 0.0000   |

# Chapter 12

## The Black-Scholes Formula

### Question 12.2

| N | Call | Put |
|---|------|-----|
| 8 | 3.464 | 1.718 |
| 9 | 3.361 | 1.642 |
| 10 | 3.454 | 1.711 |
| 11 | 3.348 | 1.629 |
| 12 | 3.446 | 1.705 |

The observed values are slowly converging toward the Black-Scholes values of the example. Please note that the binomial solution oscillates as it approaches the Black-Scholes value.

### Question 12.4

a)

| T | Call Price |
|---|-----------|
| 1 | 18.6705 |
| 2 | 18.1410 |
| 5 | 15.1037 |
| 10 | 10.1571 |
| 50 | 0.2938 |
| 100 | 0.0034 |
| 500 | 0.0000 |

The benefit to holding the call option is that we do not have to pay the strike price and that we continue to earn interest on the strike. On the other hand, the owner of the call option forgoes the dividend payments he could receive if he owned the stock. As the interest rate is zero and the dividend yield is positive, the cost of holding the call outweighs the benefits.

b)

| T | Call Price |
|---|---|
| 1 | 18.7281 |
| 2 | 18.2284 |
| 5 | 15.2313 |
| 10 | 10.2878 |
| 50 | 0.3045 |
| 100 | 0.0036 |
| 500 | 0.0000 |

Although the call option is worth marginally more when we introduce the interest rate of 0.001, it is still not enough to outweigh the cost of not receiving the huge dividend yield.

## Question 12.6

a) Using the Black-Scholes formula, we find a call-price of $16.33.

b) We determine the one-year forward price to be:

$$F_{0,T}(S) = S \times \exp(r \times T) = \$100 \times \exp(0.06 \times 1) = \$106.1837$$

c) As the textbook suggests, we need to set the dividend yield equal to the risk-free rate when using the Black-Scholes formula. Thus:

$$C(106.1837, 105, 0.4, 0.06, 1, \mathbf{0.06}) = \$16.33$$

This exercise shows the general result that a European futures option has the same value as the European stock option provided the futures contract has the same expiration as the stock option.

## Question 12.8

a) We have to be careful here: Now we have to take into account the dividend yield when calculating the nine-month forward price:

$$F_{0,T}(S) = S \times \exp[(r - delta) \times T] = \$100 \times \exp[(0.08 - 0.03) \times 0.75] = \$103.8212.$$

b) Having found the correct forward price, we can use equation (12.7) to price the call option on the futures contract: $C(103.8212, 95, 0.3, 0.08, 0.75, \mathbf{0.08}) = \$14.3863$

c) The price we found in part (b) and the prices of the previous question are identical. 12.7(a), 12.7(b), and 12.8(b) are all based on the same Black-Scholes formula, only the way in which we input the variables differs.

# Question 12.10

Time decay is measured by the Greek letter *theta*. We will show in the following that the statement of the exercise is not always correct.

We assume $S = 50$, sigma $= 0.3$, $r = 0.08$, delta $= 0$, $K = 40$, 50 and 60, and $T = 1$ month, 3 months, ..., 13 months.

We can calculate:

| K = 40 Time expiration | to Theta | Call price | Dollar change | Perc. change |
|---|---|---|---|---|
| 1 month | −0.010 | 10.271 | −0.010 | −0.09% |
| 3 months | −0.012 | 10.939 | −0.012 | −0.11% |
| 5 months | −0.012 | 11.678 | −0.012 | −0.11% |
| 7 months | −0.012 | 12.409 | −0.012 | −0.10% |
| 9 months | −0.012 | 13.115 | −0.012 | −0.09% |
| 11 months | −0.011 | 13.792 | −0.011 | −0.08% |
| 13 months | −0.011 | 14.443 | −0.011 | −0.07% |

| K = 50 | Theta | Call price | Dollar change | Perc. change |
|---|---|---|---|---|
| 1 month | −0.034 | 1.892 | −0.034 | −1.82% |
| 3 months | −0.022 | 3.481 | −0.022 | −0.63% |
| 5 months | −0.018 | 4.669 | −0.018 | −0.39% |
| 7 months | −0.016 | 5.688 | −0.016 | −0.28% |
| 9 months | −0.015 | 6.606 | −0.015 | −0.22% |
| 11 months | −0.014 | 7.453 | −0.014 | −0.18% |
| 13 months | −0.013 | 8.247 | −0.013 | −0.16% |

| K = 60 | Theta | Call price | Dollar change | Perc. change |
|---|---|---|---|---|
| 1 month | −0.004 | 0.037 | −0.004 | −11.14% |
| 3 months | −0.012 | 0.577 | −0.012 | −2.01% |
| 5 months | −0.013 | 1.319 | −0.013 | −0.97% |
| 7 months | −0.013 | 2.088 | −0.013 | −0.61% |
| 9 months | −0.012 | 2.846 | −0.012 | −0.44% |
| 11 months | −0.012 | 3.586 | −0.012 | −0.34% |
| 13 months | −0.012 | 4.306 | −0.012 | −0.27% |

Please note that we measure theta as the dollar change in the call value per day. Therefore, we divided the returned value of the Excel function BSTheta by 360.

We can see that, in fact, the statement of the exercise is not correct. Only the at-the-money call option ($K = 50$) has a monotonically decreasing theta (in time) and thus the greatest time decay for short expirations (i.e., a decreasing dollar and percentage price change if we reduce the time to maturity by one day). Both the out-of-the-money and in-the-money option have thetas that are not monotonically decreasing in time to maturity, and neither the dollar change nor the percentage change are necessarily greater the shorter the time to expiration is.

In-the-money and out-of-the-money options can have thetas that are increasing in time to maturity, as the following figure, graphing the theta of the above options, depending on time to maturity, shows:

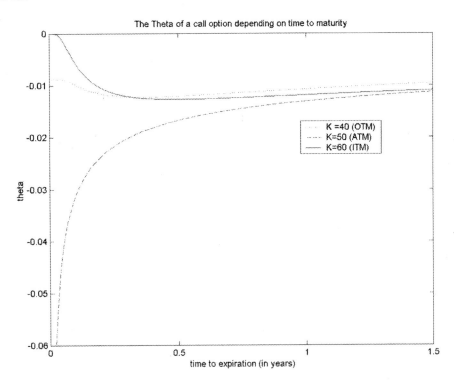

## Question 12.12

| epsilon | call_u | call_d | div_appr. |
|---------|--------|--------|-----------|
| 0.0010 | 14.3364 | 14.4363 | −0.4997 |
| 0.0100 | 13.8923 | 14.8917 | −0.4997 |
| 0.1000 | 9.9457 | 19.9526 | −0.5003 |

Let's do a quick check: $C(\dots, \text{delta} = 0.03) = 14.3863$, $C(\dots, \text{delta} = 0.04) = 13.8923$. The difference is −0.4940, which is very close to our approximation of −0.4997.

## Question 12.14

a) The Greeks of the bull spread are simply the sum of the Greeks of the individual options. The Greeks of the call with a strike of 45 enter with a negative sign because this option was sold.

|       | Bought Call(40) | Sold Call(45) | Bull Spread |
|-------|-----------------|---------------|-------------|
| Price | 4.1553 | −2.1304 | 2.0249 |
| Delta | 0.6159 | −0.3972 | 0.2187 |
| Gamma | 0.0450 | −0.0454 | −0.0004 |
| Vega | 0.1081 | −0.1091 | −0.0010 |
| Theta | −0.0136 | 0.0121 | −0.0014 |
| Rho | 0.1024 | −0.0688 | 0.0336 |

b)

|       | Bought Call(40) | Sold Call(45) | Bull Spread |
|-------|-----------------|---------------|-------------|
| Price | 7.7342 | −4.6747 | 3.0596 |
| Delta | 0.8023 | −0.6159 | 0.1864 |
| Gamma | 0.0291 | −0.0400 | −0.0109 |
| Vega | 0.0885 | −0.0122 | −0.0331 |
| Theta | −0.0137 | 0.0152 | 0.0016 |
| Rho | 0.1418 | −0.1152 | 0.0267 |

c) Because we simultaneously buy and sell an option, the graphs of gamma, vega, and theta have inflection points (see graph below). Therefore, the initial intuition one may have had—that the Greeks should be symmetric at $S = \$40$ and $S = \$45$—is not correct.

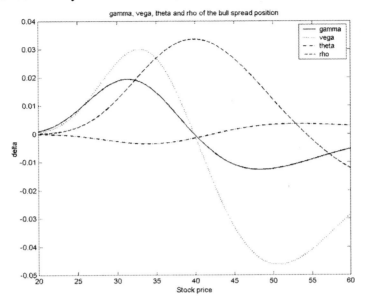

gamma, vega, theta and rho of the bull spread position

## Question 12.16

a) one day to expiration

| S | call delta | put delta | call vega | put vega | call theta | put theta | call rho | put rho |
|---|---|---|---|---|---|---|---|---|
| 60 | 0.000 | −1.000 | 0.000 | 0.000 | 0.000 | 0.022 | 0.000 | −0.003 |
| 65 | 0.000 | −1.000 | 0.000 | 0.000 | 0.000 | 0.022 | 0.000 | −0.003 |
| 70 | 0.000 | −1.000 | 0.000 | 0.000 | 0.000 | 0.022 | 0.000 | −0.003 |
| 75 | 0.000 | −1.000 | 0.000 | 0.000 | 0.000 | 0.022 | 0.000 | −0.003 |
| 80 | 0.000 | −1.000 | 0.000 | 0.000 | 0.000 | 0.022 | 0.000 | −0.003 |
| 85 | 0.000 | −1.000 | 0.000 | 0.000 | 0.000 | 0.022 | 0.000 | −0.003 |
| 90 | 0.000 | −1.000 | 0.000 | 0.000 | 0.000 | 0.022 | 0.000 | −0.003 |
| 95 | 0.001 | −0.999 | 0.000 | 0.000 | −0.002 | 0.021 | 0.000 | −0.003 |
| 100 | 0.509 | −0.491 | 0.021 | 0.021 | −0.326 | −0.304 | 0.001 | −0.001 |
| 105 | 0.999 | −0.001 | 0.000 | 0.000 | −0.025 | −0.003 | 0.003 | 0.000 |
| 110 | 1.000 | 0.000 | 0.000 | 0.000 | −0.022 | 0.000 | 0.003 | 0.000 |
| 115 | 1.000 | 0.000 | 0.000 | 0.000 | −0.022 | 0.000 | 0.003 | 0.000 |
| 120 | 1.000 | 0.000 | 0.000 | 0.000 | −0.022 | 0.000 | 0.003 | 0.000 |
| 125 | 1.000 | 0.000 | 0.000 | 0.000 | −0.022 | 0.000 | 0.003 | 0.000 |
| 130 | 1.000 | 0.000 | 0.000 | 0.000 | −0.022 | 0.000 | 0.003 | 0.000 |
| 135 | 1.000 | 0.000 | 0.000 | 0.000 | −0.022 | 0.000 | 0.003 | 0.000 |
| 140 | 1.000 | 0.000 | 0.000 | 0.000 | −0.022 | 0.000 | 0.003 | 0.000 |

ab) one year to expiration

| S | call delta | put delta | call vega | put vega | call theta | put theta | call rho | put rho |
|---|---|---|---|---|---|---|---|---|
| 60 | 0.099 | −0.901 | 0.105 | 0.105 | −0.006 | 0.015 | 0.052 | −0.871 |
| 65 | 0.154 | −0.846 | 0.154 | 0.154 | −0.008 | 0.012 | 0.086 | −0.837 |
| 70 | 0.220 | −0.780 | 0.207 | 0.207 | −0.012 | 0.009 | 0.131 | −0.792 |
| 75 | 0.294 | −0.706 | 0.258 | 0.258 | −0.015 | 0.006 | 0.184 | −0.739 |
| 80 | 0.372 | −0.628 | 0.303 | 0.303 | −0.018 | 0.002 | 0.245 | −0.678 |
| 85 | 0.450 | −0.550 | 0.336 | 0.336 | −0.021 | 0.000 | 0.310 | −0.614 |
| 90 | 0.526 | −0.474 | 0.358 | 0.358 | −0.023 | −0.003 | 0.376 | −0.547 |
| 95 | 0.597 | −0.403 | 0.368 | 0.368 | −0.025 | −0.005 | 0.442 | −0.482 |
| 100 | 0.662 | −0.338 | 0.366 | 0.366 | −0.026 | −0.006 | 0.504 | −0.419 |
| 105 | 0.719 | −0.281 | 0.354 | 0.354 | −0.027 | −0.007 | 0.563 | −0.360 |
| 110 | 0.769 | −0.231 | 0.335 | 0.335 | −0.028 | −0.007 | 0.617 | −0.306 |
| 115 | 0.811 | −0.189 | 0.311 | 0.311 | −0.028 | −0.007 | 0.665 | −0.259 |
| 120 | 0.847 | −0.153 | 0.283 | 0.283 | −0.028 | −0.007 | 0.707 | −0.216 |
| 125 | 0.877 | −0.123 | 0.254 | 0.254 | −0.027 | −0.007 | 0.743 | −0.180 |
| 130 | 0.902 | −0.098 | 0.225 | 0.225 | −0.027 | −0.006 | 0.775 | −0.148 |
| 135 | 0.922 | −0.078 | 0.197 | 0.197 | −0.026 | −0.006 | 0.801 | −0.122 |
| 140 | 0.938 | −0.062 | 0.171 | 0.171 | −0.025 | −0.005 | 0.824 | −0.100 |

We can clearly see that the entries for the one day expiration table are more extreme: There is only one day left for stock price changes, so a lot of uncertainty is resolved. For example, a deep out-of-the-money call option (e.g., at a stock price of $60) is unlikely to change during one day to some price bigger than $100, so the option most likely does not pay off; therefore, its delta is zero. On the other hand, with one year to maturity left, there is a decent chance of such a change; therefore, the price of the option reacts to a one dollar increase in the stock price.

ba) Time to expiration: one day

| S | straddle delta | straddle vega | straddle theta | straddle rho |
|---|---|---|---|---|
| 60 | −1.000 | 0.000 | 0.022 | −0.003 |
| 65 | −1.000 | 0.000 | 0.022 | −0.003 |
| 70 | −1.000 | 0.000 | 0.022 | −0.003 |
| 75 | −1.000 | 0.000 | 0.022 | −0.003 |
| 80 | −1.000 | 0.000 | 0.022 | −0.003 |
| 85 | −1.000 | 0.000 | 0.022 | −0.003 |
| 90 | −1.000 | 0.000 | 0.022 | −0.003 |
| 95 | −0.999 | 0.000 | 0.019 | −0.003 |
| 100 | 0.018 | 0.042 | −0.631 | 0.000 |
| 105 | 0.998 | 0.000 | −0.027 | 0.003 |
| 110 | 1.000 | 0.000 | −0.022 | 0.003 |
| 115 | 1.000 | 0.000 | −0.022 | 0.003 |
| 120 | 1.000 | 0.000 | −0.022 | 0.003 |
| 125 | 1.000 | 0.000 | −0.022 | 0.003 |
| 130 | 1.000 | 0.000 | −0.022 | 0.003 |
| 135 | 1.000 | 0.000 | −0.022 | 0.003 |
| 140 | 1.000 | 0.000 | −0.022 | 0.003 |

bb) Time to expiration: one year

| S | straddle delta | straddle vega | straddle theta | straddle rho |
|---|---|---|---|---|
| 60 | −0.802 | 0.209 | 0.009 | −0.819 |
| 65 | −0.692 | 0.308 | 0.004 | −0.750 |
| 70 | −0.560 | 0.415 | −0.003 | −0.661 |
| 75 | −0.412 | 0.517 | −0.009 | −0.554 |
| 80 | −0.256 | 0.605 | −0.016 | −0.433 |
| 85 | −0.100 | 0.673 | −0.021 | −0.304 |
| 90 | 0.052 | 0.717 | −0.026 | −0.171 |
| 95 | 0.194 | 0.735 | −0.030 | −0.040 |
| 100 | 0.323 | 0.732 | −0.032 | 0.086 |
| 105 | 0.438 | 0.708 | −0.034 | 0.203 |
| 110 | 0.537 | 0.670 | −0.035 | 0.310 |
| 115 | 0.623 | 0.622 | −0.035 | 0.406 |
| 120 | 0.694 | 0.567 | −0.035 | 0.490 |
| 125 | 0.754 | 0.509 | −0.034 | 0.564 |
| 130 | 0.803 | 0.451 | −0.033 | 0.626 |
| 135 | 0.844 | 0.395 | −0.032 | 0.679 |
| 140 | 0.876 | 0.342 | −0.030 | 0.724 |

bc) Explanation of the one year Greeks

We need to keep in mind that we bought both a call option and a put option, both with a strike of $100. Therefore, with a stock price smaller than $100, the put option is in the money, and the call option is out of the money. This pattern helps us when we look at the Greeks: For small stock prices, delta is negative (the put dominates) and rho is negative (recall that since the put entitles the owner to receive cash, and the present value of this is lower with a higher interest rate, the rho of a put is negative). Deep in the money put options have a positive theta; therefore, for very small stock prices, we expect (and see) a positive theta of the straddle. However, once we increase the stock price, the theta of a put becomes negative; the theta becomes progressively more negative as the negative theta effects of the call are integrated. Both put and call have the same vega, and we know that vega is highest for at-the-money options.

ca)

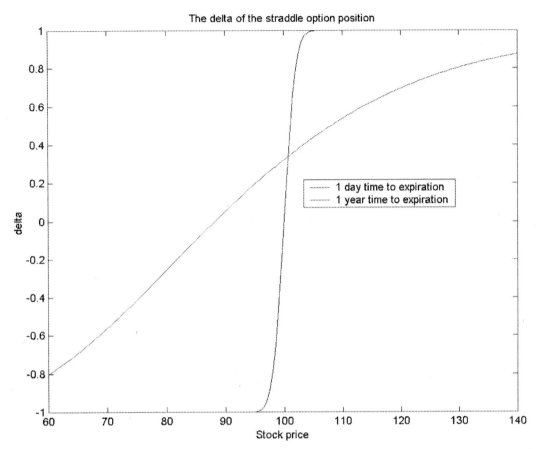

The delta of the one day time to expiration graph is a lot steeper. However, delta changes only in a small area around the strike price. With only one day to expiration left, it becomes increasingly clear whether the call option ends out of the money (delta_c = 0) and the put option ends in the money (delta_p = −1) or the call option in the money (delta_c = 1) and the put option out of the money (delta_p = 0). Taken together, this yields a delta of the straddle of either −1 or 1.

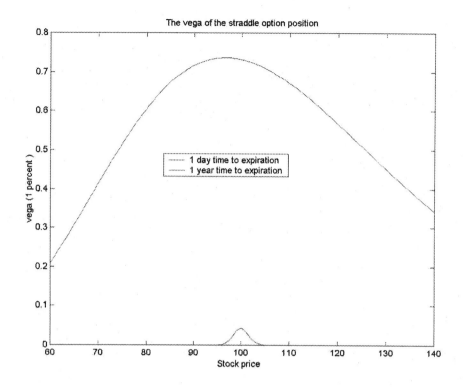

cb) Vega:

The one-day time to expiration vega graph shows only a small hump around the strike price of the option position. With only one day time to expiration left, we do not have enough time to participate in the opportunities the one percentage point increase in volatility offers to our bought straddle. However, with one year left, we see that the volatility increase has a huge effect on our straddle.

cc) Theta:

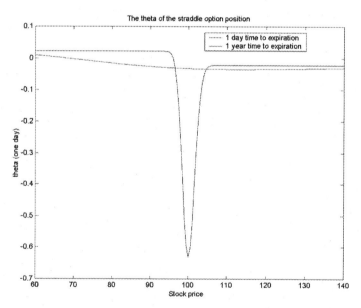

Remember, we bought a call and a put option on the same strike of $100. This figure is a nice demonstration that for bought at-the-money option positions, time decay is greatest for short time to maturity positions. Our long straddle will pay off if either the call or the put is in the money. If the current stock price is about 100 and we have only one day to expiration left, our option position will likely expire worthless. Therefore, there is a huge time decay. With longer time to maturities, chances of stock price movements away from a 100 are substantial. Therefore, the theta is much smoother and smaller.

cd) rho:

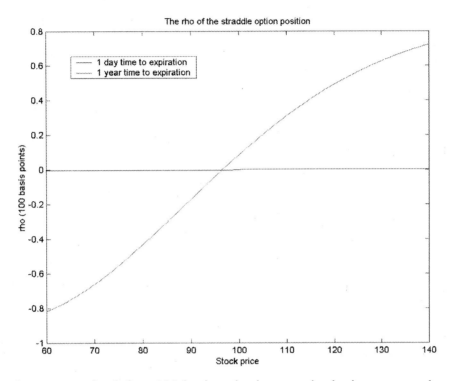

With one day to maturity left, a 100 basis point increase in the interest rate has no effect on the option position because the time we could earn interest/lose interest on the strike is just too short.

For the one year to maturity figure, we can see the following: If the stock price is higher than $100, it is the call option that is in the money, and the put expires worthless. Therefore, rho is positive (remember, rho for a call option is positive because a call entails paying the fixed strike price to receive the stock and a higher interest rate reduces the present value of the strike). For stock prices smaller than $100, the put dominates and we know that the rho of a put is negative.

## Tables for 12.18

| Inputs | | | Perpetual Options | |
|---|---|---|---|---|
| | | | Call | Put |
| Stock price | 50 | | | |
| Exercise price | 60 | Option Price | 26.35183 | 23.07471 |
| Volatility | 40.000% | Exercise at: | 317.3092 | 22.6908 |
| Risk-free interest rate | 6.000% | | | |
| Dividend yield | 3.000% | | | |

| Inputs | | | Perpetual Options | |
|---|---|---|---|---|
| | | | Call | Put |
| Stock price | 50 | | | |
| Exercise price | 60 | Option Price | 22.75128 | 23.82482 |
| Volatility | 40.000% | Exercise at: | 248.2475 | 21.75248 |
| Risk-free interest rate | 6.000% | | | |
| Dividend yield | 4.000% | | | |

| Inputs | | | Perpetual Options | |
|---|---|---|---|---|
| | | | Call | Put |
| Stock price | 50 | | | |
| Exercise price | 60 | Option Price | 27.10008 | 21.2744 |
| Volatility | 40.000% | Exercise at: | 334.9193 | 25.08067 |
| Risk-free interest rate | 7.000% | | | |
| Dividend yield | 3.000% | | | |

| Inputs | | | Perpetual Options | |
|---|---|---|---|---|
| | | | Call | Put |
| Stock price | 50 | | | |
| Exercise price | 60 | Option Price | 29.83555 | 27.62938 |
| Volatility | 50.000% | Exercise at: | 412.5475 | 17.45254 |
| Risk-free interest rate | 6.000% | | | |
| Dividend yield | 3.000% | | | |

## Question 12.18

a) The price of the perpetual call option is $26.35. It should be exercised when the stock price reaches the barrier of $317.31.

b) The price of the perpetual call option is now $22.75. It should be exercised when the stock price reaches the barrier of $248.25. The higher dividend yield makes it more costly to forgo the dividends and wait for an increase in the stock price before exercising the option. Therefore, the option is worth less, and it is optimal to exercise after a smaller increase in the underlying stock price.

c) The price of the perpetual call option is now $27.10. It should be exercised when the stock price reaches the barrier of $334.92. The higher interest rate increases the value of the call option and makes it attractive to wait a bit longer before you exercise the option, as you can continue to earn interest on the strike before you exercise. Therefore, the option is worth more, and it is only optimal to exercise after a larger increase in the underlying stock price.

d) The price of the perpetual call option is $29.84. It should be exercised when the stock price reaches the barrier of $412.55. Options love volatility. The chances of an even larger increase in the stock price are high with a large standard deviation (and your risk is capped at the downside). Therefore, the option is worth more and you wait longer until you forgo the future potential and exercise.

## Question 12.20

a) $C(100, 90, 0.3, 0.08, 1, 0.05) = 17.6988$

b) $P(90, 100, 0.3, 0.05, 1, 0.08) = 17.6988$

c) The prices are equal. This is a result of the mathematical equivalence of the pricing formulas. To see this, we need some algebra. We start from equation (12.3) of the text, the formula for the European put option:

$$P(\bullet) = \overline{K} \times \exp(-\overline{r}\,T) \times N\left(\frac{\ln\left(\frac{\overline{S}}{\overline{K}}\right) + \left(\overline{r} - \overline{\delta} - 0.5\sigma^2\right)T}{\sigma\sqrt{T}}\right) - S \times \exp(-\overline{\delta}T)$$

$$\times N\left(-\frac{\ln\left(\frac{\overline{S}}{\overline{K}}\right) + \left(\overline{r} - \overline{\delta} - 0.5\sigma^2\right)T}{\sigma\sqrt{T}}\right)$$

Now we replace:

$$\overline{K} = S, \overline{r} = \delta, \overline{\delta} = r, \overline{S} = K$$

Then:

$$= S \times \exp(-\delta T) \times N\left(\frac{\ln\left(\frac{K}{S}\right) + \left(\delta - r - 0.5\sigma^2\right)T}{\sigma\sqrt{T}}\right) - K$$

$$\times \exp(-rT) \times N\left(-\frac{\ln\left(\frac{K}{S}\right) + \left(\delta - r - 0.5\sigma^2\right)T}{\sigma\sqrt{T}}\right)$$

Since $\ln\left(\dfrac{K}{S}\right) = -\ln\left(\dfrac{S}{K}\right)$

$$= S \times \exp(-\delta T) \times N\left(\frac{\ln\left(\frac{S}{K}\right) + \left(\delta - r - 0.5\sigma^2\right)T}{\sigma\sqrt{T}}\right) - K \times \exp(-rT)$$

$$\times N\left(-\frac{\ln\left(\frac{S}{K}\right) + \left(\delta - r - 0.5\sigma^2\right)T}{\sigma\sqrt{T}}\right)$$

$$= S \times \exp(-\delta T) \times N(d_1) - K \times \exp(-rT) \times N(d_2) = C(\bullet)$$

# Chapter 13

## Market-Making and Delta-Hedging

### Question 13.2

Using the Black Scholes formula we can solve for the put premium and the put's delta: $P = 1.9905$ and $\Delta = -0.4176$. If we write this option, we will have a position that moves with the stock price. This implies our delta hedge will require shorting 41.76 shares (receiving $41.76(40) = \$1670.4$). As before, we must look at the three components of the profit. There will now be interest *earned* since we are receiving both the option premium 199.05 as well as the 1670.40 on the short sale. This $1869.43 will earn (rounding to the nearest penny) $1869.43 \times e^{0.08/365} - 1[1] = 0.41$ in interest. If the stock falls to 39 we make 41.76 on our short sale and if the stock price rises to 40.5 we lose 20.88 on our short sale. If the stock prices falls to 39 or rises to 40.5, the price of the put option we wrote will be (using $T = 90/365$) $P(39) = 2.4331$ or $P(40.5) = 1.7808$. This implies our option position will lose $243.31 - 199.05 = 44.26$ if the stock falls by \$1 and make $199.05 - 178.08 = 20.97$ if the stock rises by \$0.50. Combining these results, our profit will be

$$41.76 - 44.26 + 0.41 = -2.09 \tag{3}$$

if the stock price falls to \$39 and

$$-20.88 + 20.97 + 0.41 = 0.50. \tag{4}$$

Notice that, as in the case of the call option, the large change implies a loss and the small change involves a profit.

### Question 13.4

The 45-strike put has a premium of 5.0824 and a delta of $-0.7185$ and the 40-strike put has a premium of 1.9905 and a delta of $-0.4176$. For the put ratio spread (assume on 100 shares), our total cost is $508.24 - 200 (1.9905) = 110.14$. The delta on this position is $100 [-0.7185 - 2 (-0.4176)] = 11.67$; hence, our delta hedged requires shorting 11.67 shares (receiving $11.67(40) = \$466.80$). This implies that in one day we will receive $466.8 \, e^{0.08/365} - 1 = 0.10232 \approx 0.10$ from our short sale proceeds. Our short sale of 11.67 shares will make 11.67 if $S$ falls to 59 and will lose 5.89 if $S$ rises to 60.5. If $S$ falls to 39 in one day, the 45-strike and 40-strike puts will be worth 5.8265 and 2.4331 (respectively). This implies our put ratio spread will be worth $582.65 - (2)243.31 = 96.03$ (we lose $110.14 - 96.03 = 14.11$). If $S$ rises to 40.5 in one day, the 45-strike and 40-strike puts will be worth 4.7257 and 1.7808 (respectively), which implies the put ratio spread will be worth $472.57 - 2(178.08) = 116.41$ (we make $116.41 - 110.14 = 6.27$). Combining these three components, our profit will be

$$11.67 - 14.11 + 0.10 = -2.34 \tag{7}$$

if $S$ falls to 39 and

$$-5.89 + 6.27 + 0.10 = 0.48 \tag{8}$$

if $S$ rises to 40.5. This suggests that the put ratio spread has a negative gamma at 40.

## Question 13.6

See Table 2. Once again, note the similarities with the delta hedged call.

TABLE 2 (Problem 13.6)

| Day | 0 | 1 | 2 | 3 | 4 | 5 |
|---|---|---|---|---|---|---|
| Stock ($) | 40 | 40.642 | 40.018 | 39.403 | 38.797 | 39.42 |
| Put ($) | 199.05 | 172.66 | 196.53 | 222.60 | 250.87 | 220.07 |
| Option Delta | -0.4176 | -0.3768 | -0.4173 | -0.4592 | -0.5020 | -0.4594 |
| Investment ($) | -1869.433 | -1704.224 | -1866.514 | -2031.895 | -2198.561 | -2031.022 |
| Interest ($) | | 0.41 | 0.37 | 0.41 | 0.45 | 0.48 |
| Capital Gain ($) | | -0.42 | -0.35 | -0.40 | -0.45 | -0.48 |
| Daily Profit | | -0.01 | 0.02 | 0.01 | 0.00 | 0.00 |

## Question 13.8

See Table 4. Note the errors are larger the farther out we go as the theta will be changing. With the one day the error is minimal at $S = 40$ because $S$ does not vary and little error due to our theta approximation for it doesn't change much during the day. For five days, there is a theta error at $S_{5/365} = 40$ (of 0.0003) due to theta decreasing during the five days.

TABLE 4 (Problem 13.8)

| Future S | 1 day Approx | 1 day Actual | 5 days Approx | 5 days Actual | 25 days Approx | 25 days Actual | Errors 1d | Errors 5d | Errors 25d |
|---|---|---|---|---|---|---|---|---|---|
| 25.00 | 13.4458 | 13.5091 | 13.4257 | 13.5389 | 13.3256 | 13.6910 | -0.0634 | -0.1132 | -0.3655 |
| 25.50 | 12.9188 | 13.0236 | 12.8988 | 13.0524 | 12.7986 | 13.2004 | -0.1048 | -0.1537 | -0.4018 |
| 26.00 | 12.4032 | 12.5414 | 12.3831 | 12.5692 | 12.2830 | 12.7123 | -0.1382 | -0.1861 | -0.4293 |
| 26.50 | 11.8989 | 12.0631 | 11.8789 | 12.0897 | 11.7787 | 12.2273 | -0.1642 | -0.2109 | -0.4486 |
| 27.00 | 11.4059 | 11.5892 | 11.3859 | 11.6146 | 11.2857 | 11.7458 | -0.1833 | -0.2287 | -0.4600 |
| 27.50 | 10.9243 | 11.1204 | 10.9043 | 11.1443 | 10.8041 | 11.2685 | -0.1961 | -0.2400 | -0.4644 |
| 28.00 | 10.4541 | 10.6573 | 10.4340 | 10.6796 | 10.3339 | 10.7960 | -0.2033 | -0.2456 | -0.4621 |
| 28.50 | 9.9951 | 10.2005 | 9.9751 | 10.2211 | 9.8749 | 10.3289 | -0.2054 | -0.2460 | -0.4540 |
| 29.00 | 9.5475 | 9.7507 | 9.5275 | 9.7694 | 9.4273 | 9.8680 | -0.2031 | -0.2419 | -0.4407 |
| 29.50 | 9.1113 | 9.3084 | 9.0913 | 9.3253 | 8.9911 | 9.4140 | -0.1971 | -0.2340 | -0.4229 |
| 30.00 | 8.6864 | 8.8744 | 8.6663 | 8.8892 | 8.5662 | 8.9675 | -0.1880 | -0.2229 | -0.4013 |
| 30.50 | 8.2728 | 8.4492 | 8.2528 | 8.4619 | 8.1526 | 8.5293 | -0.1764 | -0.2091 | -0.3767 |
| 31.00 | 7.8706 | 8.0335 | 7.8505 | 8.0440 | 7.7504 | 8.1000 | -0.1630 | -0.1935 | -0.3497 |
| 31.50 | 7.4797 | 7.6278 | 7.4596 | 7.6361 | 7.3595 | 7.6805 | -0.1482 | -0.1765 | -0.3210 |
| 32.00 | 7.1001 | 7.2327 | 7.0801 | 7.2387 | 6.9799 | 7.2712 | -0.1325 | -0.1586 | -0.2913 |
| 32.50 | 6.7319 | 6.8485 | 6.7119 | 6.8523 | 6.6117 | 6.8728 | -0.1166 | -0.1404 | -0.2611 |
| 33.00 | 6.3750 | 6.4758 | 6.3550 | 6.4773 | 6.2548 | 6.4860 | -0.1008 | -0.1223 | -0.2312 |
| 33.50 | 6.0295 | 6.1150 | 6.0095 | 6.1143 | 5.9093 | 6.1111 | -0.0855 | -0.1048 | -0.2018 |
| 34.00 | 5.6953 | 5.7663 | 5.6753 | 5.7634 | 5.5751 | 5.7486 | -0.0710 | -0.0882 | -0.1736 |
| 34.50 | 5.3724 | 5.4301 | 5.3524 | 5.4251 | 5.2522 | 5.3990 | -0.0576 | -0.0727 | -0.1468 |
| 35.00 | 5.0609 | 5.1064 | 5.0409 | 5.0994 | 4.9407 | 5.0625 | -0.0455 | -0.0585 | -0.1218 |
| 35.50 | 4.7607 | 4.7956 | 4.7407 | 4.7867 | 4.6405 | 4.7394 | -0.0349 | -0.0460 | -0.0989 |
| 36.00 | 4.4719 | 4.4976 | 4.4519 | 4.4869 | 4.3517 | 4.4299 | -0.0257 | -0.0350 | -0.0782 |
| 36.50 | 4.1944 | 4.2125 | 4.1744 | 4.2001 | 4.0742 | 4.1340 | -0.0181 | -0.0257 | -0.0599 |
| 37.00 | 3.9282 | 3.9403 | 3.9082 | 3.9263 | 3.8080 | 3.8519 | -0.0121 | -0.0181 | -0.0438 |
| 37.50 | 3.6734 | 3.6809 | 3.6534 | 3.6655 | 3.5532 | 3.5834 | -0.0075 | -0.0121 | -0.0302 |
| 38.00 | 3.4299 | 3.4341 | 3.4099 | 3.4174 | 3.3097 | 3.3285 | -0.0042 | -0.0075 | -0.0187 |
| 38.50 | 3.1978 | 3.1998 | 3.1777 | 3.1820 | 3.0776 | 3.0870 | -0.0020 | -0.0043 | -0.0094 |
| 39.00 | 2.9770 | 2.9778 | 2.9569 | 2.9590 | 2.8568 | 2.8587 | -0.0008 | -0.0020 | **-0.0019** |
| 39.50 | 2.7675 | 2.7677 | 2.7475 | 2.7481 | 2.6473 | 2.6433 | -0.0002 | -0.0006 | 0.0040 |
| 40.00 | 2.5694 | 2.5694 | 2.5493 | 2.5490 | 2.4492 | 2.4406 | **0.0000** | **0.0003** | 0.0085 |
| 40.50 | 2.3826 | 2.3824 | 2.3626 | 2.3615 | 2.2624 | 2.2502 | 0.0002 | 0.0011 | 0.0122 |
| 41.00 | 2.2071 | 2.2064 | 2.1871 | 2.1851 | 2.0869 | 2.0717 | 0.0007 | 0.0020 | 0.0152 |
| 41.50 | 2.0430 | 2.0411 | 2.0230 | 2.0195 | 1.9228 | 1.9047 | 0.0019 | 0.0035 | 0.0181 |
| 42.00 | 1.8903 | 1.8860 | 1.8702 | 1.8643 | 1.7701 | 1.7488 | 0.0042 | 0.0060 | 0.0213 |
| 42.50 | 1.7488 | 1.7408 | 1.7288 | 1.7190 | 1.6286 | 1.6034 | 0.0080 | 0.0098 | 0.0252 |
| 43.00 | 1.6187 | 1.6051 | 1.5987 | 1.5833 | 1.4985 | 1.4682 | 0.0137 | 0.0154 | 0.0304 |
| 43.50 | 1.5000 | 1.4783 | 1.4800 | 1.4567 | 1.3798 | 1.3426 | 0.0217 | 0.0233 | 0.0372 |
| 44.00 | 1.3926 | 1.3602 | 1.3726 | 1.3388 | 1.2724 | 1.2262 | 0.0324 | 0.0338 | 0.0461 |
| 44.50 | 1.2965 | 1.2502 | 1.2765 | 1.2291 | 1.1763 | 1.1186 | 0.0463 | 0.0474 | 0.0578 |
| 45.00 | 1.2118 | 1.1480 | 1.1917 | 1.1273 | 1.0916 | 1.0191 | 0.0638 | 0.0645 | 0.0725 |
| 45.50 | 1.1384 | 1.0531 | 1.1184 | 1.0328 | 1.0182 | 0.9273 | 0.0853 | 0.0855 | 0.0908 |
| 46.00 | 1.0763 | 0.9651 | 1.0563 | 0.9454 | 0.9561 | 0.8429 | 0.1112 | 0.1109 | 0.1133 |
| 46.50 | 1.0256 | 0.8837 | 1.0056 | 0.8645 | 0.9054 | 0.7652 | 0.1420 | 0.1411 | 0.1402 |
| 47.00 | 0.9862 | 0.8084 | 0.9662 | 0.7898 | 0.8660 | 0.6940 | 0.1779 | 0.1764 | 0.1721 |
| 47.50 | 0.9582 | 0.7388 | 0.9382 | 0.7209 | 0.8380 | 0.6286 | 0.2194 | 0.2173 | 0.2094 |
| 48.00 | 0.9415 | 0.6747 | 0.9215 | 0.6574 | 0.8213 | 0.5689 | 0.2668 | 0.2640 | 0.2524 |
| 48.50 | 0.9362 | 0.6156 | 0.9161 | 0.5990 | 0.8160 | 0.5143 | 0.3205 | 0.3171 | 0.3017 |
| 49.00 | 0.9421 | 0.5612 | 0.9221 | 0.5454 | 0.8219 | 0.4644 | 0.3809 | 0.3767 | 0.3575 |
| 49.50 | 0.9595 | 0.5113 | 0.9394 | 0.4961 | 0.8393 | 0.4190 | 0.4482 | 0.4433 | 0.4203 |
| 50.00 | 0.9881 | 0.4654 | 0.9681 | 0.4509 | 0.8679 | 0.3776 | 0.5227 | 0.5172 | 0.4903 |
| 50.50 | 1.0281 | 0.4233 | 1.0081 | 0.4095 | 0.9079 | 0.3400 | 0.6048 | 0.5986 | 0.5679 |
| 51.00 | 1.0795 | 0.3847 | 1.0594 | 0.3716 | 0.9593 | 0.3059 | 0.6947 | 0.6878 | 0.6534 |
| 51.50 | 1.1421 | 0.3494 | 1.1221 | 0.3370 | 1.0219 | 0.2750 | 0.7927 | 0.7851 | 0.7470 |
| 52.00 | 1.2162 | 0.3171 | 1.1961 | 0.3054 | 1.0960 | 0.2469 | 0.8990 | 0.8907 | 0.8490 |
| 52.50 | 1.3015 | 0.2876 | 1.2815 | 0.2765 | 1.1813 | 0.2216 | 1.0139 | 1.0049 | 0.9597 |
| 53.00 | 1.3982 | 0.2607 | 1.3782 | 0.2502 | 1.2780 | 0.1986 | 1.1375 | 1.1279 | 1.0794 |
| 53.50 | 1.5062 | 0.2362 | 1.4862 | 0.2263 | 1.3860 | 0.1780 | 1.2701 | 1.2599 | 1.2081 |
| 54.00 | 1.6256 | 0.2138 | 1.6056 | 0.2045 | 1.5054 | 0.1593 | 1.4118 | 1.4011 | 1.3461 |
| 54.50 | 1.7563 | 0.1934 | 1.7363 | 0.1847 | 1.6361 | 0.1425 | 1.5629 | 1.5516 | 1.4936 |
| 55.00 | 1.8984 | 0.1749 | 1.8784 | 0.1667 | 1.7782 | 0.1274 | 1.7235 | 1.7116 | 1.6508 |

Note that the error of 0.0003 is not constant across the range of prices. Besides the familiar delta-gamma error (i.e., ignoring third order changes of $S$), there is the effect changes in $S$ have on $\Theta$ (technically the cross partial derivative $\partial^2 f(S, t)/(\partial S \partial t)$). The delta gamma error is symmetric; however, this cross partial error is not symmetric. To see this, we can use the fundamental theorem of calculus on the Black Scholes formula. By put call parity, the put and call will have the same second cross partial derivative which is equal to

$$\frac{\partial^2 f(S,t)}{\partial S \partial t} = -\Delta_{call} \frac{r - \sigma^2/2}{\sqrt{T-t}} \tag{9}$$

In this case this, $r - \sigma^2/2 > 0$ and $\Delta_{call} > 0$; hence, the above term is negative; this implies our approximation does not include terms like $\frac{\partial^2 f(S,t)}{\delta S \delta t}(\Delta S)(\Delta t)$, which will be positive when $S < 40$ and negative when $S_T > 40$; hence, our approximation will underestimate the option value for low $S_T$ and overestimate it for large $S_T$.

# Question 13.10

See Figures 2 & 3.

Figure 2 (Problem 13.10)

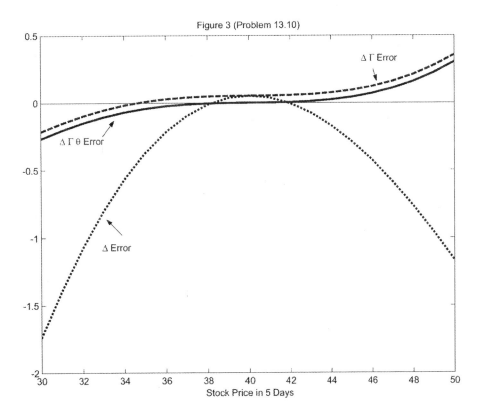

Figure 3 (Problem 13.10)

## Question 13.12

See Figures 5 and 6.

Figure 5 (Problem 13.12)

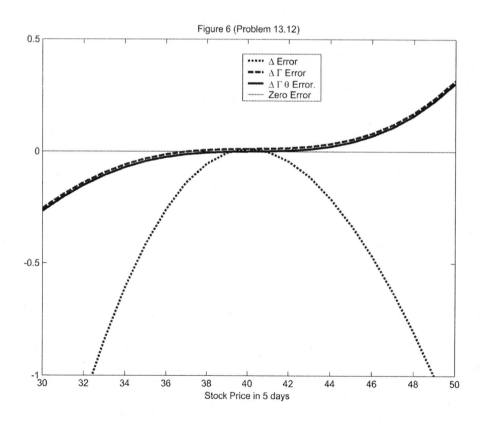

Figure 6 (Problem 13.12)

## Question 13.14

Using the given parameters, a six-month 45-strike put has a price and Greeks of $P = 5.3659$, $\Delta = -0.6028$, $\Gamma = 0.045446$, and $\Theta_{\text{per day}} = -0.0025$. Note that $\Theta$, as given in the software, is per day. Equation (13.9) uses annualized rates (i.e., $\Theta h$ is in the equation). Hence for equation (13.9) we should use $-0.9139$. For equation (13.9), we have a market-maker profit of

$$-\left( \frac{0.09}{2} 40^2 (0.045446) - 0.9139 + 0.08[(-0.6028)40 - 5.3659] \right) h \qquad (12)$$

$$= -(3.2721 - 0.9139 - 2.3582)\, h = 0. \qquad (13)$$

## Question 13.16

For our 45-strike put that we've written: $P_1 = 5.3596$, $\Delta_1 = -0.6051$, $\Gamma_1 = 0.0457$. The 40-strike has $C_2 = 4.1217$, $\Delta_2 = 0.6151$, $\Gamma_2 = 0.0454$. Since we are "short" gamma (we wrote an option), we must buy $\Gamma_1/\Gamma_2 = 0.0457/0.0454 = 1.007$ 40-strike calls. Our option position will have a total delta of $0.6051 + (1.007)\, 0.6151 = 1.2245$; hence, we have to short 1.2247 shares. Our total initial cash flow will be $5.3596 - 1.007(4.1217) + 1.2247\,(40) = 50.20$. Using primes to denote next day prices, our one-day profit will be

$$-P_1' - 1.007C_2' + 1.2247S' - 50.208e^{0.08/365} \qquad (15)$$

We use Black Scholes with $T - t = 179/365$ to arrive at our profit in Figure 8.

Figure 8 (Problem 13.16)

## Question 13.18

The relevant values of the spread are: $f = 5.0824 - 2(1.9905) = 1.1014$, $\Delta = -0.71845 - 2(-0.4176) = 0.11675$, and $\Gamma = 0.05633 - 2(0.06516) = -0.07399$. Since we wrote the spread, to $\Gamma$ hedge we need to buy $0.07399/0.04536 = 1.6312$ options. The delta of the spread and the call will become $0.11675 + (1.6312)(0.6151) = 1.120$; therefore, we need to short 1.120 shares. The graph of our profit is given in Figure 10.

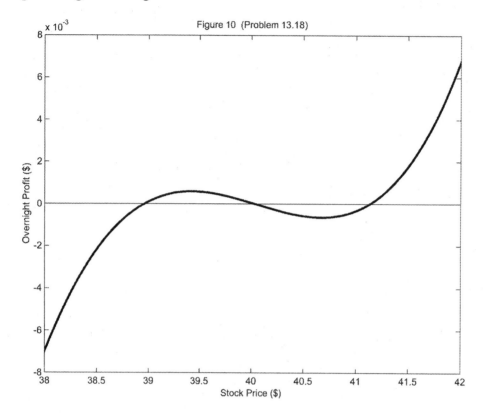

Figure 10 (Problem 13.18)

## Question 13.20

We purchased a 91-day, 40-strike call, denoted option 1.

a) Using a 180-day, 40-strike call (option 2) to delta-rho hedge we must write 50.64 of these options and short 27.09 shares of stock. Our one day profit is given in Figure 13.

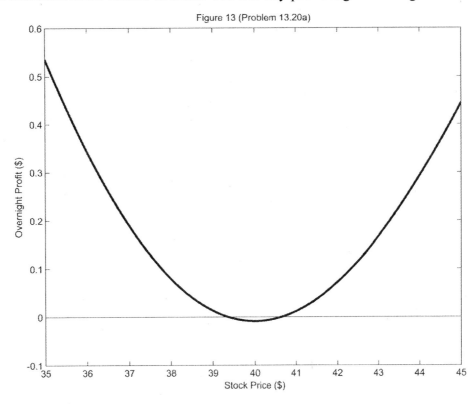

Figure 13 (Problem 13.20a)

b) Using option 2 as well as a one-year (365 day) 45-strike put (option 3) to delta-gamma-vega hedge, we have the following solution: $n_2 = -1.2259$, $n_3 = -0.2874$, and $n_S = 0.0307$. The one-day profit is given in Figure 14 on the next page. If we added another option, call it option 4, we can try to hedge all of the Greeks (note $\Theta$ will be taken care of by the Black-Scholes Equation). Let vega be noted by $v$

$$\Delta_2 n_2 + \Delta_3 n_3 + \Delta_4 n_4 + n_S = -0.5824 \tag{16}$$

$$\Gamma_2 n_2 + \Gamma_3 n_3 + \Gamma_4 n_4 = -0.0652 \tag{17}$$

$$v_2 n_2 + v_3 n_3 + v_4 n_4 = -0.0780 \tag{18}$$

$$Rho_2 n_2 + Rho_3 n_3 + Rho_4 n_4 = -0.0511 \tag{19}$$

These are four equations and four unknowns (the coefficients are from the Black-Scholes model). Note we must try to solve the last three equations simultaneously, which give us the position of the three options, and then use the underlying asset to delta hedge.

On a related note, occasionally you will find strange things may happen when we use options with the same maturity. For a given time to maturity, vega and gamma are proportional (i.e., $v_i = k_i \Gamma_i$). If two options have the same time to maturity, then $k_1 = k_2$. If we use option 2 to gamma hedge a position of option 1, $\Gamma_2 n_2 = -n_1 \Gamma_1$; with the same maturity, we have

$$v_2 n_2 = k_2 \Gamma_2 n_2 = -k_1 n_1 \Gamma_1 = -n_1 v_1. \tag{20}$$

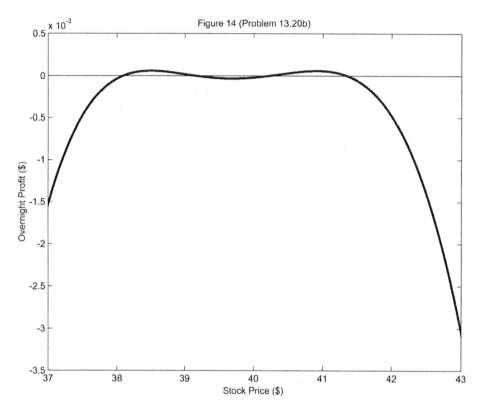

Figure 14 (Problem 13.20b)

Hence gamma hedging takes care of vega hedging if the maturity matches. Similarly, if we use two options (call the 2 and 3) of the same maturity to hedge an option (call it 1) position with a different maturity, we will have a problem for $\Gamma_2 n_2 + \Gamma_3 n_3 = -n_1 \Gamma_1$ implies

$$v_2 n_2 + v_3 n_3 = k_2 (\Gamma_2 n_2 + \Gamma_3 n_3) = -k_2 n_1 \Gamma_1 = -\left(\frac{k_2}{k_1}\right) n_1 v_1. \tag{21}$$

If $k_1 = k_2$ (i.e., the option being hedged is different from the two traded options' identical time to maturity), it will be impossible to both gamma and vega hedge. A simple algebraic way of looking at this is by trying to solve

$$ax + by = c \tag{22}$$

$$2(ax + by) = kc \tag{23}$$

Unless $k = 2$ (in which case we have an infinite number of solutions), there will be no solution.

# Chapter 14

## Exotic Options: I

### Question 14.2

The arithmetic average is 5 (three 5s, one 4, and one 6) and the geometric average is $(5 \times 4 \times 5 \times 6 \times 5)^{1/5} = 4.9593$. For the next sequence, the arithmetic average does not change ($= 5$); however, the geometric average, $(3 \times 4 \times 5 \times 6 \times 7)^{1/5} = 4.7894$ is much lower. As the standard deviation increases (holding arithmetic means constant), the geometric return decreases. As an example, suppose we have two observations, $1 + \sigma$ and $1 - \sigma$. The arithmetic mean will be 1; however, the geometric mean will be $\sqrt{(1+\sigma)(1-\sigma)} = \sqrt{1-\sigma^2} < 1$.

### Question 14.4

Using the forward tree specification, $u = \exp(0.08/2 + 0.3/\sqrt{2}) = 1.2868$, $d = \exp(0.08/2 - 0.3/\sqrt{2}) = 0.84187$, and risk neutral probability $p = (e^{0.08/2} - d)/(u - d) = 0.44716$. The two possible prices in six months are 128.68 and 84.19; the three possible one-year prices are 165.58, 108.33, and 70.87.

Using the 6m and 12m prices, the possible arithmetic averages are (in one year) are 147.13, 118.50, 96.26, and 77.53. The four possible geometric averages are 145.97, 118.07, 95.50, and 77.24. These are in the order: u-u, u-d, d-u, and d-d.

a) The four intrinsic values will be $165.58 - 147.13 = 18.45$ (u-u), 0 (u-d), $108.33 - 96.26 = 12.07$ (d-u), and zero (d-d). This will give an up value of $e^{-0.04}p18.45 = 7.93$, a down value of $e^{-0.04}p12.07 = 5.19$, and an initial value of $e^{-0.04}(p7.93 + (1 - p)5.19) = 6.1602$.

b) The four intrinsic values will be $165.58 - 145.97 = 19.61$ (u-u), zero (u-d), $108.33 - 95.50 = 12.83$ (d-u), and zero (d-d). This will give an up value of $e^{-0.04}p19.61 = 8.43$ and a down value of $e^{-0.04}p12.83 = 5.51$ with an initial value of $e^{-0.04}(p8.43 + (1 - p)5.51) = 6.55$.

### Question 14.6

a) A standard call is worth 4.1293.

b) A knock in call will also be worth 4.1293 (you can verify this with the software). In order for the standard call to ever be in the money, it must pass through the barrier. They, therefore, give identical payoffs.

c) Similar reasoning implies the knock-out will be worthless since in order for $S_T > 45$, the barrier must have been hit making knocking out the option.

## Question 14.8

See Table Three for the prices and ratio. The longer the time to expiration, the greater the dispersion of $S_T$. For the standard put option, this increases the value unless the option expiration starts to become large (we lose time value of receiving the strike price). For the knock-out, there is an extra negative effect a higher expiration date has. With higher dispersion of $S_T$, the greater chance for larger $S_T$, the greater the chance of being knocked out; however, there will also be a higher chance for the barrier to be hit.

Table Three (Problem 14.8)

| T | Standard | Knock-Out | Ratio |
|---|---|---|---|
| 0.25 | 5.0833 | 3.8661 | 1.3148 |
| 0.5 | 5.3659 | 3.4062 | 1.5753 |
| 1 | 5.6696 | 2.8626 | 1.9806 |
| 2 | 5.7862 | 2.2233 | 2.6025 |
| 3 | 5.6347 | 1.8109 | 3.1115 |
| 4 | 5.3736 | 1.5094 | 3.5601 |
| 5 | 5.0654 | 1.2761 | 3.9695 |
| 100 | 0.0012 | 0.0001 | 24.4951 |

## Question 14.10

When $K = 0.9$, the only scenarios where the up and out puts have a different payoff than the standard put is where the exchange rate rises to the barrier of 1 (or 1.05) before six months (i.e., $x_t > 1$ for $t < T$) and then end below 0.9 (i.e., $x_T < 0.9$). In this case, the up and out puts will pay nothing (they will have gotten knocked out) and the standard put will pay the intrinsic value $0.9 - x_T$. Given the volatility assumption, these scenarios are virtually impossible, and for the small chance that they happen, the payoff in for the standard put would be small.

When $K = 1$ the scenarios mentioned above are much more likely as $x$ only has to rise above 1 (or 1.05) and then finish below 1. With higher time to expirations, the probabilities of such scenarios will become nonnegligible and we should expect the up and out to have lower values than the standards (when $K = 0.9$).

## Question 14.12

a) 3.6956

b) In one year, the put option will be worth more than $2 if $S_1 < 44.35$.

c) 2.2978

d) If we buy the standard put from part (a) as well as this compound option for $x$, we will keep the standard put if $S_1 < 44.35$ and sell it for $2 otherwise. This identical to putting $2e^{-0.08}$ in the risk free bond and buying the compound option in part (c). The total costs must be identical implying $3.6956 + x = 2.2978 + 2e^{-0.08}$, implying $x = 0.448$.

## Question 14.14.

Using $\sigma = 30\%$, $r = 8\%$, and $\delta = 0$. See Figure 2 on the next page. When we are close to maturity (e.g., $T = 1/52$) we see large variations in delta. The discontinuity at $K_2$ can require deltas greater than one. The value of the option can go from close to zero to close to $10 with little movement in the price (if $S_T$ is close to $K_1$). If $T \pm 0$, delta will be close zero for $S < 100$, enormous for $S = 100$, and close to one if $S > 100$. This problem does not occur as $T$ becomes larger.

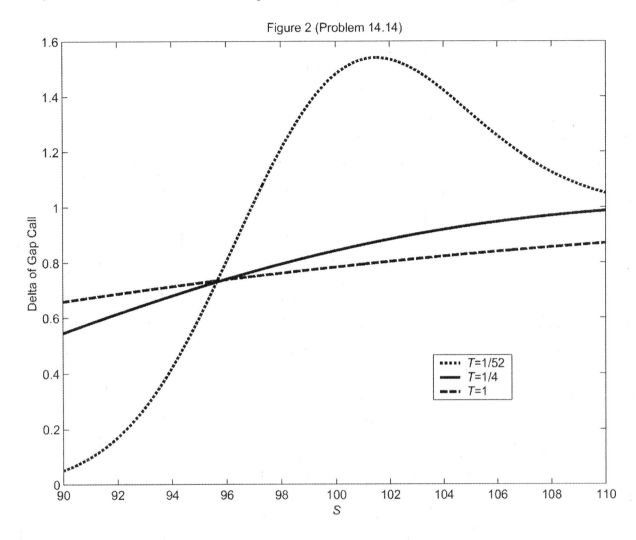

Figure 2 (Problem 14.14)

## Question 14.16

Under Black-Scholes, the standard 40-strike call on $S$ will be

$$BSCall\,(40, 40, 0.3, 0.08, 1, 0). \tag{2}$$

For the exchange option on $S$ using two thirds of a share of $Q$ as the strike, we use a strike of $(2/3)\,60 = 40$, a volatility of $\sqrt{0.3^2 + 0.5^2 - 2(0.5)(0.3)(0.5)} = 0.43589$, and an "interest rate" of $0.04$:

$$BSCall\,(40, 40, 0.43589, 0.04, T, 0). \tag{3}$$

For all but very long time to maturities, the higher volatility will offset the lower "interest" and the exchange option will be worth more. With $T = 1$, we have the standard option is worth 6.28, and the exchange option is worth 7.58.

## Question 14.18

a) *Var* $[\ln (S/Q)] = 0.3^2 + 0.3^2 - 2\,(0.3)\,(0.3) = 0$ and the option is worthless (it will never be in the money as $S_T = Q_T$).

b) *Var* $[\ln (S/Q)] = 0.3^2 + 0.4^2 - 2\,(0.3)\,(0.4) = 0.01$ hence we use a 10 percent volatility in Black-Scholes. With $T = 1$, we have the exchange option equal to \$1.60.

c) If $\ln (S)$ and $\ln (Q)$ are jointly normal with $\rho = 1$, then they are linearly related. Hence,

$$\ln (Q) = \ln (40)\left(1 - \frac{\sigma_Q}{\sigma_S}\right) + \frac{\sigma_Q}{\sigma_S}\ln(S). \tag{4}$$

In part (a), $\ln (Q) = \ln (S) \Rightarrow Q = S$. For part (b),

$$\ln (Q) = \frac{\ln(40)}{3} + \frac{4}{3}\ln (S) \Rightarrow 0.2924S^{4/3}. \tag{5}$$

If $S$ rises (say $S_T = 50$), then $Q$ will be greater than $S$ (say $Q_T = 53.861$); the option will be in the money if $S$ falls because $Q$ will fall by a greater amount, making the exchange option have value.

## Question 14.20

a) Since the options will be expiring at $t_1$, we have the payoff of a put if $S_T < K$ and the payoff of a call if $S_T > K$. This is equivalent to a $K$ strike straddle.

b) Using put-call parity at $t_1$, the value of the as-you-like-it option at $t_1$ will be:

$$\left(\max C\left(S_1, K,\ T-t_1\right), C\left(S_1, K, T-t_1\right)\ + Ke^{-r(T-t_1)} - Se^{-\delta(T-t_1)}\right) \tag{6}$$

$$= C\left(S_1, K,\ T-t_1\right)\ +\ \max\left(0, Ke^{-r(T-t_1)} - Se^{-\delta(T-t_1)}\right) \tag{7}$$

$$= C\left(S_1, K, T-t_1\right) + e^{-\delta(T-t_1)}\max\left(0, Ke^{(\delta-r)(T-t_1)} - S\right). \tag{8}$$

The first term is the value of a call with strike $K$ and maturity $T$ ; the second term is the payoff from holding $e^{-\delta(T-t_1)}$ put options that expire at $t_1$ with strike $Ke^{(\delta-r)(T-t_1)}$ .

## Question 14.22

a) $6.0831

b) The current price of a 1m 95-strike put is 1.2652. In fact, a 1m put with a strike equal to 95 percent of the stock price will always be equal to 1.2652 percent of the stock price. Therefore, the present value of twelve of these 1m 95 percent strike puts is 12 (1.2652) = 15.182.

c) Technically, and perhaps nonintuitively, the rolling insurance strategy costs more because it is more expensive to replicate. Note that one strategy doesn't dominate another. If the price never falls less than 5 percent in month, all twelve of the one-month options will be worthless; yet the price in one year could have fallen by more than 5 percent. Interest aside, the rollover options will give the holder $\sum_{i=0}^{11}\max\left(S_{i+1} - 0.95S_i, 0\right)$; whereas, the simple insurance gives the holder max($S_{12}$ − 0.95$S_0$, 0). The rollover strategy has the advantage of being able to provide payoffs (insurance) for each month regardless of the past. If the stock price rises in one month to (say) $120, the simple insurance option will be less effective whereas the rollover will provide a new insurance option with a strike of 0.95 (120) = 114.

# Chapter 15

## Financial Engineering and Security Design

### Question 15.2

For this problem let $B = \frac{1}{1.03}$ .

a)  The prepaid forward price is $1{,}200e^{-0.015(3)} = 1{,}147.20$.

b)  We have to solve the coupon, $c$, that solves

$$c\left(\sum_{i=1}^{6} B^i\right) + 1{,}147.20 = 1{,}200 \Rightarrow c = 52.8\left(\frac{1-B}{B-B^7}\right) = 9.7467. \tag{3}$$

c)  The prepaid forward price for one share at time $t$ is $F_t^P = 1{,}200e^{-0.015t}$ ; for each semiannual share, we can write the relevant prepaid forward price as $1{,}200D_i$ where $D = e^{-0.015/2}$. With this formulation we have a similar analysis for the fractional shares, $c^*$:

$$c^*\left(\sum_{i=1}^{6} D^i\right)1{,}200 + 1{,}147.20 = 1{,}200 \Rightarrow c^* = \frac{52.8}{1{,}200}\left(\frac{1-D}{D-D^7}\right) = 0.007528 \text{ shares}. \tag{4}$$

Note this is interpreted as we will receive 0.007528 units of the index every six months. This has a current value of $1{,}200(0.007528) = 9.0336$. We could quote $c^*$ in dollars (\$9.0336) instead of units.

### Question 15.4

The relevant two year interest rate is $\ln (1/0.8763) /2 = 6.6\%$.

a)  The embedded option is worth 247.88. The prepaid forward is worth $1{,}200e^{-0.015(2)} = 1{,}164.53$. The bond price is worth the sum $1{,}164.53 + 247.88 = 1{,}412.41$.

b)  $\lambda$ must solve $1{,}164.53 + \lambda 247.88 = 1{,}200 \Rightarrow \lambda = 35.47/247.88 = 0.1431$.

### Question 15.6

We continue to use 6.6 percent as the relevant two-year interest rate.

a)  The out of the money option (i.e., $K = 1{,}500$) is worth 141.54, making the bond have a value of $1{,}164.53 + 247.88 - 141.54 = 1{,}270.9$.

b)  We must solve $1{,}164.53 + \lambda (247.88 - 141.54) = 1{,}200$ for a solution of $\lambda = 0.3336$.

c)  If $\lambda = 1$, we have to adjust the strike (from part (a), we know we have to lower $K$ ) to make the out of the option worth $C(K) = 1{,}164.53 + 247.88 - 1{,}200 = 212.41 \Rightarrow K \approx 1{,}284$.

## Question 15.8

Using a semiannual coupon of $c$, if the value of the CD is 1,300, $c$ and $\gamma$ must solve

$$1{,}300 = 1{,}300 e^{-0.06 \times 5.5} + c \left( \sum_{i=1}^{11} e^{-0.03i} \right) + \gamma 441.44. \tag{9}$$

This implies the participation rate, as a function of $c$ is $\gamma = 0.82774 - 0.0209c$ (i.e., a line with intercept 0.82774 and slope $-0.0209$). For example, a \$10 semiannual coupon will require 0.618 74 call options to have the CD be worth 1,300. If the bank would like to earn 5 percent, $c$ and $\gamma$ must solve

$$1{,}300\,(1 - 0.05) = 1{,}300 e^{-0.06 \times 5.5} + c \left( \sum_{i=1}^{11} e^{-0.03i} \right) + \gamma 441.44. \tag{10}$$

This implies $\gamma = 0.6805 - 0.0209c$; this is a parallel line (to the previous answer's line) with a lower intercept.

## Question 15.10

The 2,600-strike call has a value of 162.48. The 1,300-strike put is worth 178.99. This implies $\lambda$ must solve

$$1{,}300 = 1{,}300 e^{-0.06 \times 5.5} - 178.99 + \lambda\,(162.48) \tag{12}$$

implying $\lambda = 3.3505$.

## Question 15.12

See Table One for the numerical solution.

Table One (Problem 15.12)

|        |   | 0.06 | 0.06 | 0.06 | 0.05 | 0.07 | 0.06 | 0.06 |
|--------|---|------|------|------|------|------|------|------|
|        | $r$ | 0.06 | 0.06 | 0.06 | 0.05 | 0.07 | 0.06 | 0.06 |
|        | $\sigma$ | 0.3 | 0.2 | 0.4 | 0.3 | 0.3 | 0.3 | 0.3 |
|        | $\delta$ | 0.015 | 0.015 | 0.015 | 0.015 | 0.015 | 0.005 | 0.025 |
| 15.12a | $V$ | 1243.61 | 1183.16 | 1304.37 | 1278.54 | 1211.64 | 1280.15 | 1210.12 |
| 15.12b | $\gamma$ | 0.7000 | 0.8702 | 0.5850 | 0.6160 | 0.7684 | 0.6260 | 0.7851 |

a)  The value is $1{,}300 e^{-r \times 5.5} + 0.7 \times BSCall\,(1300, 1300, \sigma, r, 5.5, \delta)$.

b)  We must solve for $\gamma$,

$$1{,}300(1 - 0.043) = 1{,}300 e^{-r \times 5.5} + \gamma \times BSCall\,(1300, 1300, \sigma, r, 5.5, \delta) \tag{13}$$

## Question 15.14

The two-year, prepaid forward price is 17.351.

a) $c^*$ must solve

$$c^*20.5\,(0.9388) + c^*19.8\,(0.8763) + 19.8\,(0.8763) = 20.9 \tag{15}$$

Hence $c* = \dfrac{20.9-17.351}{19.245+17.351} = 0.097$ barrels. In dollars, this is currently worth $0.097\,(20.9) =$ $\$2.0273$.

b) Similarly,

$$c^*\left(\sum_{i=1}^{8} F_{t_i}^{P}\right) = 20.9 - 17.351 \tag{16}$$

hence $c_* = \dfrac{20.9-17.351}{152.1556} = 0.023325$ barrels, currently worth $0.0233\,(20.9) = \$0.4875$.

## Question 15.16

For the options, we can use the following answer from part (a) as the underlying in the nondividend *BSCall*, the interest rate being $\ln\,(1/0.9388) = 6.32\%$.

a) The prepaid forward price is $F_i\,P_i = 20.5\,(0.9388) = 19.2454$.

b) With $K_1 = 19.577$ and $K_2 = 21.577$, a put with $K_1$ strike is worth 0.7436 and a call with strike $K_2$ is worth the same. Hence the cost is the same as the prepaid forward contract, 19.2454. With this contract, we receive the spot price of oil if $S_1$ is between 19.577 and 21.577. We receive a lower bound of 19.577 (if $S_1 < 19.577$) and an upper bound of 21.577 (if $S_1 > 21.577$). This payoff is similar to a bull spread with a risk free bond. The prepaid forward has the holder owning a barrel of oil; whereas, this contract involves owning a barrel of oil only if $S_1$ is between $K_1$ and $K_2$. It will do worse than the prepaid forward if $S_1 > K_2$ and better if $S_1 < K_1$ (trading off upside to protect downside).

c) The value of this claim is zero: $S_1 - 20.50$ is a (zero cost) forward contract and the two options have equal premiums. If $S_1$ is between $K_1$ and $K_2$, we pay 20.5 and receive a barrel of oil worth $S_1$. If $S_1 < K_1 = 19.577$, we pay 20.5, receive a barrel of oil, and sell it for $K_1$ leading to a cash flow of $19.577 - 20.5 = -0.923$. If $S_1 > K_2 = 21.577$, we pay 20.5, receive a barrel of oil, and sell it for $K_2$ leading to a cash flow of $21.577 - 20.5 = 1.077$. This is the profit from a bull spread.

## Question 15.18

Since the contract has zero value, it doesn't matter which side of the contract we examine. Consider the "seller" of the contract. Each quarter $i$, the seller receives a cash flow

$$19.90 - \overline{F} + \max(S_i - 19.90, 0) - \max(S_i - 21.90, 0) \tag{17}$$

To check, if $S_i < 19.90$, the seller has a cash flow $19.90 - \overline{F}$. If $S_i$ is between 19.90 and 21.90, there is a cash flow of $S_i - \overline{F}$, and if $S_i > 21.90$, the cash flow if $21.90 - \overline{F}$. Each quarter the bull spread will have a value

$$V_i = BSCall(F_iP_i, 19.90, 0.15, r_i, t_i, 0) - BSCall(F_iP_i, 21.90, 0.15, r_i, t_i, 0) \tag{18}$$

where $P_i$ is zero coupon bond price from Problems Table and $e^{r_i t_i} = P_i$. Table Two on the next page shows the values for $V_i$ and $r_i$. We now must solve for $\overline{F}$ in

$$V_{contract} = 0 = \sum_{i=1}^{8}\left(19.90 - \overline{F}\right)P_i + \sum_{i=1}^{8}V_i \tag{19}$$

implying

$$\overline{F} = \frac{\sum_{i=1}^{8}V_i}{\sum_{i=1}^{8}P_i} + 19.90 = \frac{6.3616}{7.4475} + 19.90 = 20.754. \tag{20}$$

Table Two (Problem 15.18)

| Quarter | 1 | 2 | 3 | 4 | 5 | 6 | 7 | 8 |
|---|---|---|---|---|---|---|---|---|
| F | 21 | 21.1 | 20.8 | 20.5 | 20.2 | 20 | 19.9 | 19.8 |
| P | 0.9852 | 0.9701 | 0.9546 | 0.9388 | 0.9231 | 0.9075 | 0.8919 | 0.8763 |
| F*P | 20.6892 | 20.46911 | 19.85568 | 19.2454 | 18.64662 | 18.15 | 17.74881 | 17.35074 |
| r | 0.059642 | 0.060712 | 0.06195 | 0.063153 | 0.064014 | 0.064708 | 0.065372 | 0.066023 |
| V of Spread | 1.00798 | 1.00023 | 0.880993 | 0.791487 | 0.718889 | 0.675769 | 0.653802 | 0.632465 |

## Question 15.20

The main textbook gives the following table of payment at maturity of the Times Mirror PEPS:

| Underlying price of Netscape at expiration | | Payoff to DECS holder |
|---|---|---|
| S(T) | <$39.25 | S(T) |
| $39.25 < S(T) | < $45.14 | $39.25 |
| $45.14 < S(T) | | $39.25 + 0.8696 × (S(T) − $45.14) |

The above table can be replicated with the following instruments: buy one share of Netscape, sell one Netscape call with a strike of $39.25, and buy 0.8696 calls with a strike of $45.14.

Furthermore, we need to take care of the dividends of the PEPS. We are entitled to the annual cash dividend of $1.67 (which is the issue price of $39.25 times the coupon rate of 4.25 percent) of the PEPS (which is missing from the above strategy). We therefore need to add zero-coupon bonds characterizing the PEPS dividend payments.

$$P_{PEPS} = S_T - C(39.25,\ldots) + 0.8696 \times C(45.14) + PV(Div_{PEPS})$$

We can value the annual PEPS dividend

| | | P(t) | disc. DECS Div |
|---|---|---|---|
| R | 0.07 | | |
| PEPS | | | |
| Div | 1.668125 | | |
| 1 | | 0.932 | 1.555 |
| 2 | | 0.869 | 1.450 |
| 3 | | 0.811 | 1.352 |
| 4 | | 0.756 | 1.261 |
| 5 | | 0.705 | 1.176 |
| | | | 6.794 |

Therefore, we can solve: $P_{PEPS} = 39.25 - 16.302 + 0.8696 \times 18.153 + 6.794 = 42.067$. The PEPS is worth $42.067 today.

## Question 15.22

a) We have to value a forward contract with a dividend yield of zero. We know that the price for such a forward contract is:

$$F_{0,T} = S_0 \times \exp(rt) = 100 \times \exp(0.03 \times 3) = 109.417$$

b) We could see in part (a) that the forward price is taking into account the interest accruing to the $100. The annual payment, if the price agreed upon is $100, would reflect that interest. The coupon would have to be 3 percent, continuously compounded, or $3.045, at the end of Years 1, 2, and 3.

c) Now, we can depict the payoff of the stock purchase contract as follows:

| Underlying stock price at expiration | Payoff to stock purchase contract holder |
|---|---|
| S(T) < $100.00 | $1 \times S(T)$ |
| $100 \le S(T) < $116.20 | $S(T) + (\$100 - S(T)) = \$100$ |
| $\dfrac{\$100}{\$116.20} \le S(T)$ | $S(T) + (\$100 - S(T)) + 100/116.20 \times (S(T) - \$116.20)$ |

Therefore, we can value this complicated stock purchase contract as a simple stock purchase contract for a price of $100 plus the simultaneous purchase of 100/116.20 call options with a strike of 116.20 and a sale of one call option with a strike of $100. We valued the simple stock purchase contract in part (b), and now have to value the two stock options:

Based on the information given in the exercise, we obtain:

$$C(100) = 24.2068$$

$$C(116.20) = 18.1729$$

Overall, we have:

$$Payoff = S_T - 100 + \max(0, S_T - 100) + \frac{100}{116.20} \times \max(0, S_T - 116.20)$$

and a price today of:

$$\text{Price} = -\sum_{t=1}^{3} \$3.045 \times \exp(-0.03 \times t) + 24.2068 - 0.8606 \times 18.1729$$

$$= -8.6056 + 24.2068 - 15.6396$$

$$= -\$0.0384$$

We would need to be paid 3.84 cents to enter into the contract.

d) Now, we are not entitled to receive the dividend the stock pays. This is an inconvenience, and we have to take this into account when calculating the forward price:

$$F_{0,T} = S_0 \times \exp[(r - \delta) \times t] = 100 \times \exp[(0.03 - 0.03) \times 3] = 100.00$$

$100 is now the fair price, and we would not have to pay a coupon in part (b). For part (c), we would pay up to $24.2068 - 15.6396 = 8.5672$ to enter the stock purchase contract with the contractual features described.

# Chapter 16

## Corporate Applications

### Question 16.2

Let $K$ be the maturity value of the debt. Equity is valued as a call option with strike $K$ on the assets $A = 100$, with the given interest and volatility. By Black-Scholes, the four values of equity will be $E = 5.9977$, $11.4278$, $23.3041$, and $37.0374$; debt will be $D = 100 - E = 94.0023$, $88.5722$, $76.6959$, and $62.9626$. Yields are given by $De^{yT} = K$ which implies $y = \ln(K/D)/T = 0.3042$, $0.2118$, $0.1495$, and $0.1245$. The debt to equity ratios are $D/E = 15.6732$, $7.7506$, $3.2911$, and $1.7000$.

### Question 16.4

The value and delta of the relevant five-year call option is $E = 34.6653$ and $\beta = 0.7453$. Using equation (16.8), the expected return on equity is

$$r_E = 0.08 + (0.12 - 0.08)\frac{100(0.7453)}{34.6653} = 16.60\%. \tag{1}$$

The volatility of equity is given by

$$\sigma_E E = \Delta\sigma_A A \Rightarrow \sigma_e = \frac{\Delta\sigma_A A}{E} = \frac{100(0.3)(0.7453)}{34.6653} = 64.50\%. \tag{2}$$

Alternatively, since

$$r_E = r + \frac{(r_A - r)}{\sigma_A}\sigma_E, \tag{3}$$

we can solve

$$\sigma_E = \sigma_A\frac{r_E - r}{r_A - r} = 0.3\frac{0.086}{0.04} = 64.5\%. \tag{4}$$

See Figures One, Two, and Three for the effect on expected returns when we vary $A$, $\sigma$, and $r$. For changes in $r$, we assume that $r_A$ changes by the same amount (i.e., the risk premium on assets is constant at $r_A - r = 4\%$).

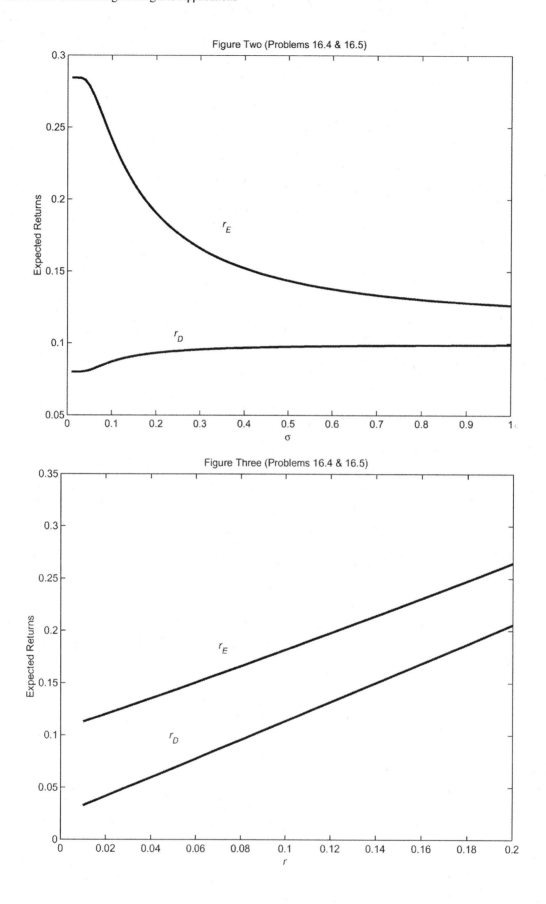

Figure Two (Problems 16.4 & 16.5)

Figure Three (Problems 16.4 & 16.5)

## Question 16.6

a)  $y = \ln (100/D) /5 = 0.1585, 0.0853, 0.0678, 0.0627,$ and $0.0600$.

b)  See Table Three.

Table Three (Problem 16.6b)

| Volatility | Yield on Debt |
|---|---|
| 0.10 | 0.0653 |
| 0.15 | 0.0732 |
| 0.20 | 0.0825 |
| 0.25 | 0.0926 |
| 0.30 | 0.1034 |
| 0.35 | 0.1148 |
| 0.40 | 0.1266 |
| 0.45 | 0.1390 |
| 0.50 | 0.1519 |
| 0.55 | 0.1652 |
| 0.60 | 0.1791 |
| 0.65 | 0.1934 |
| 0.70 | 0.2082 |
| 0.75 | 0.2236 |
| 0.80 | 0.2394 |
| 0.85 | 0.2557 |
| 0.90 | 0.2725 |
| 0.95 | 0.2898 |
| 1.00 | 0.3077 |

## Question 16.8

Let $V$ be the market value of the new project, and let $k$ be the cost of the project ($V - k$ would be the NPV). If the project is paid for with junior debt of face value $F$, then the junior debt must be worth $k$; this implies

$$\text{Junior Debt Value} = C (100 + V, 150) - C (100 + V, 150 + F) = k. \qquad (7)$$

Shareholders wealth, if they do the project, will be $C (100 + V, 150 + F)$. Hence the change in their wealth is

$$C (100 + V, 150 + F) - C(100, 150) = C (100 + V, 150) - C(100, 150) - k. \qquad (8)$$

$C (100, 150) = 26.0672$ is the initial value of shareholders wealth. When $k = 1$, shareholders' wealth would rise if $C (100 + V, 150) > 26.0672 + 1 \Rightarrow V > 1.5806$. When $k = 10$, shareholders wealth would rise if $V > 14.9817$. When $k = 25$, shareholders wealth would rise if $V > 35.1288$. These are solved numerically; you can use $\Delta$ (and $\Gamma$) to approximate them algebraically.

## Question 16.10

Using equation (16.12):

a)  $(20/22)BSCall(5, 15, 0.3, 0.08, 5, 0) = 0.3209$ per share, which is 0.6418 in total.

b)  $(20/35)BSCall(5, 20, 0.3, 0.08, 10, 0) = 0.5601$ per share, which is 15 (0.5601) = 8.4015 in total.

## Question 16.12

The debt is worth $D = A - BSCall(100, 200, 0.30, 0.08, 10, 0) = 60.1035$. The warrants are worth $\frac{20}{28} BSCall\left(\frac{100}{20}, 25, 0.30, 0.08, 10, 0\right) = 0.5191$ per share which is 8 (0.5191) = 4.1528 in total. Equity is the residual, $E = 100 - 60.1035 - 4.1528 = 35.744$ or 35.744/20 = 1.7872 per share.

## Question 16.14

The risk-free bond has a value of $1,000 \times \exp(-0.06 \times 5) = 740.818$.

The stock price calculated in Example 16.5 in the main textbook is $11.809. The strike price of the option is $M/q = 1,000/50 = 20$.

Hence, the fifty call options have a value of $50 \times BSCall$ (11.809, 20, 0.30, 0.06, 5, 0) = 109.156.

The total "naïve" value is: 740.818 + 109.156 = 849.974, which is about $30 smaller than the value of $879.39 calculated in Example 16.5 of the main textbook.

## Question 16.16

The expected number of years to exercise is computed as $1(0.1) + 2(0.1) + 3(0.8) = 2.7$. If we use 2.7 years as the time to expiration in the Black-Scholes formula, we get a price of $BSCall(100, 100, 0.3, 0.08, 2.7, 0) = 28.91$. The Black-Scholes premiums for one, two, and three years to expiration are 15.71 (one year), 24.02 (two years), and 30.85 (three years). The expected value of the options is

$$0.1\ (15.71) + 0.1\ (24.02) + 0.8\ (30.85) = 28.65. \tag{17}$$

The answer is different depending upon whether we use the average time to maturity to compute an option price, or whether we compute the average option price. The second procedure—averaging the option values with different times to maturity—is correct. To see this, imagine that we have a large number of executives with options who have identical probabilities of survival and option grants. If the group were large enough, we could be sure that 10 percent of the executives would die each of the first two years, and 80 percent would exercise after three years. Since the company has given options to the executives, it has a short position in call options. The company could hedge its obligation to this group of executives by buying 10 percent one-year options, 10 percent two-year options, and 80 percent three-year options. This yields an option cost per executive of 28.65. The 2.7-year option, by contrast, is a fiction that does not correspond to anything real.

## Question 16.18

These are forward start options. Each option has time to maturity of five years. Since there are no dividends, receiving a five-year ATM option in $t$ years is equivalent to receiving a five-year ATM option today. Hence, we can add them up (they all have the same value),

$$Value = 30000BSCall\,(100, 100, 0.30, 0.08, 5, 0) = \$1,260,340. \tag{18}$$

## Question 16.20

a) This makes the amount paid (as a function of $S_A$) continuous at the collar points: 1.714 (35) = 60 and 1.333 (45) = 60; 1.714 = 60/35 and 1.333 = 60/45.

b) The deal can be looked at as giving Company B's shareholders 1.333 shares of A, a short position on 1.714 of 35-strike puts, and a long position of 1.333 of 45-strike puts. If $S_A > 45$, both options are out of the money, and we have 1.333 shares of A. If $35 \leq S_A \leq 45$, we sell our 1.333 shares for $45. If $S_A \leq 35$, we sell our 1.333 shares for 45 but have to buy 1.714 shares for 35. By design, see the previous answer, these amounts are the same (we receive 60 and pay 60). We are now left with 1.714 shares of company $B$. The value of this offer is

$$\frac{4}{3}\left[S_A + P\,(45)\right] - \frac{60}{35}P\,(35) = \frac{4}{3}(47.3422) - \frac{60}{35}2.4283 = 58.96. \tag{19}$$

c) For volatilities ranging from 20 percent to more than 60 percent, the value stays between 58.65 and 59.

## Question 16.22

We can value the options using the Black-Scholes spreadsheet and the inputs given in the text. We have:

$$Call(44.50, 44.50, 0.566, 0.06, 4.9, 0) = 24.31243$$
$$Call(63.25, 63.25, 0.566, 0.06, 4.9, 0) = 34.55642$$
$$Call(63.25, 44.50, 0.566, 0.06, 4.9, 0) = 40.11634$$

Note that for the Black-Scholes formula we have: 63.25/44.50 * Call(44.50, 44.50) = Call(63.25, 63.25).

Ms. Tagliaferro does not seem to understand option pricing. From the above results, it is evident that the stock price around the grant matters very much for the cost to the company. Most likely, Ms. Tagliaferro confuses intrinsic value and true option price. It is true that the intrinsic value to the employee is zero before the options vest because he cannot get the money.

However, the company should be concerned with its cost, which is measured by the Black-Scholes price.

If the board knew about the earnings surprise when they granted the option package (which is very likely), they wasted a lot of their shareholders' money. Their decision to give the CEO a 44.50 at-the-money option grant when they knew the stock price would rise to 63.25 cost shareholders $[C(63.25, 44.50) - C(63.25, 63.25)] * 600,000 = \$3,335,952$.

## Question 16.24

The following spreadsheet contains the answer:

| Inputs | | | | |
|---|---|---|---|---|
| **Stock price** | 100 | | **h** | 1 |
| **Strike Price** | 100 | | **u** | 1.3499 |
| **Volatility** | 30% | | **d** | 0.7408 |
| **Domestic r** | 0.05 | | **exp(r\*h)** | 1.0513 |
| **Dividend** | 0 | | **exp(divyld\*h)** | 1 |
| **Time to Maturity** | 3 | | **Prob up** | 0.5097 |
| **0=Forward tree;** | | | | |
| **1=CRR** | 1 | | **Prob Down** | 0.4903 |

**Stock price process:**

| | | | |
|---|---|---|---|
| 100.00 | 134.99 | 182.21 | 245.96 |
| | 74.08 | 100.00 | 134.99 |
| | | 54.88 | 74.08 |
| | | | 40.66 |

**Intrinsic value**

| | | | |
|---|---|---|---|
| 0.00 | 34.99 | 82.21 | 145.96 |
| | 0.00 | 0.00 | 34.99 |
| | | 0.00 | 0.00 |
| | | | 0.00 |

**One-period value**

| | | | |
|---|---|---|---|
| 16.96 | 39.86 | 87.09 | 0.00 |
| | 0.00 | 16.96 | 0.00 |
| | | 0.00 | 0.00 |
| | | | 0.00 |

**Two-period value**

| | | |
|---|---|---|
| 19.33 | 50.14 | 87.09 |
| | 8.23 | 16.96 |
| | | 0.00 |

**Reported Expense**

| | | |
|---|---|---|
| 19.33 | 10.28 | 0.00 |
| | 8.23 | 0.00 |
| | | 0.00 |

**PV(expense)**

| | | |
|---|---|---|
| 28.1473078 | 10.2759199 | 0.00 |
| | 8.22549925 | 0.00 |
| | | 0.00 |

The present value of the option deductions is 28.147, as was to be shown. Remember that you have to compare the two-period value of 50.14 against the one-period value of 39.86.

# Chapter 17

## Real Options

### Question 17.2

If you invest at time $T$, you receive (at time $T$) an "NPV"

$$NPV_T = \frac{0.8(1.02)^{T+1}}{1.05} + \frac{0.8(1.02)^{T+2}}{1.05^2} - 1.5 - 1.5 \tag{5}$$

$$= (1.02)^T X - 1.5 \tag{6}$$

where $X = 0.8 (1.02/1.05) + 0.8 (1.02/1.05)_2$. This is growing at a decreasing rate; we can show this by looking at the growth rate

$$g_t = \frac{NPV_{t+1} - NPV_t}{NPV_t} = \frac{0.02}{1\left(\frac{1.5}{X(1.02)^t}\right)}. \tag{7}$$

Notice $g_0 = 0.02/ (1 - 1.5/X) = 0.955$, and as $t$ gets very large, $g_t$ approaches 0.02. The key insight is that if we invest in the machine, you will be receiving the NPV and this cash grows at 5 percent (the risk-free rate). Therefore, it is not optimal for you to invest if the NPV is growing at a higher rate (i.e., if $g_t > 5\%$ then you should not invest). If $g_t < 5\%$, you should have invested. Therefore, we need to solve $g_T = 5\%$ for the optimal time $T$ to invest:

$$\frac{0.02}{1\left(\frac{1.5}{X(1.02)^t}\right)} = 0.05 \Rightarrow T = 24.727 \text{ years.} \tag{8}$$

The NPV (today's NPV) is

$$\frac{X(1.02)^{24.727} - 1.5}{1.05^{24.727}} = 0.29926. \tag{9}$$

The harder way to do this problem is to maximize the log of the NPV directly.

$$\ln(NPV) = \ln\left(\frac{X(1.02)^T - 1.5}{1.05^T}\right), \tag{10}$$

which is a calculus exercise (set the derivative equal to zero). The answer ($NPV = 0.29931$ and $T = 25.224$) will be slightly off due to using simple interest rates.

# Question 17.4

See Table One.

Table One (Problem 17.4)

| Year (*t*) | Widget Price | NPV at *t* | NPV of Policy |
|---|---|---|---|
| 0 | | 27.00 | 27.00 |
| 1 | 0.55 | 29.20 | 27.81 |
| 2 | 0.57 | 31.49 | 28.56 |
| 3 | 0.59 | 33.87 | 29.26 |
| 4 | 0.62 | 36.34 | 29.90 |
| 5 | 0.64 | 38.92 | 30.49 |
| 6 | 0.67 | 41.59 | 31.04 |
| 7 | 0.70 | 44.38 | 31.54 |
| 8 | 0.72 | 47.27 | 32.00 |
| 9 | 0.75 | 50.28 | 32.41 |
| 10 | 0.78 | 53.41 | 32.79 |
| 11 | 0.81 | 56.67 | 33.13 |
| 12 | 0.85 | 60.06 | 33.44 |
| 13 | 0.88 | 63.58 | 33.72 |
| 14 | 0.92 | 67.24 | 33.96 |
| 15 | 0.95 | 71.05 | 34.18 |
| 16 | 0.99 | 75.01 | 34.36 |
| 17 | 1.03 | 79.13 | 34.53 |
| 18 | 1.07 | 83.42 | 34.66 |
| 19 | 1.11 | 87.88 | 34.78 |
| 20 | 1.16 | 92.51 | 34.87 |
| 21 | 1.21 | 97.33 | 34.94 |
| 22 | 1.25 | 102.35 | 34.99 |
| 23 | 1.30 | 107.56 | 35.02 |
| **24** | **1.36** | **112.98** | **35.03** |
| **25** | **1.41** | **118.62** | **35.03** |
| 26 | 1.47 | 124.49 | 35.01 |
| 27 | 1.52 | 130.59 | 34.98 |
| 28 | 1.59 | 136.93 | 34.93 |
| 29 | 1.65 | 143.53 | 34.87 |

| Year (*t*) | Widget Price | NPV at *t* | NPV of Policy |
|---|---|---|---|
| 30 | 1.72 | 150.39 | 34.80 |
| 31 | 1.78 | 157.52 | 34.71 |
| 32 | 1.86 | 164.94 | 34.62 |
| 33 | 1.93 | 172.66 | 34.51 |
| 34 | 2.01 | 180.69 | 34.39 |
| 35 | 2.09 | 189.03 | 34.27 |
| 36 | 2.17 | 197.72 | 34.14 |
| 37 | 2.26 | 206.74 | 34.00 |
| 38 | 2.35 | 216.13 | 33.85 |
| 39 | 2.44 | 225.90 | 33.69 |
| 40 | 2.54 | 236.06 | 33.53 |
| 41 | 2.64 | 246.62 | 33.36 |
| 42 | 2.75 | 257.60 | 33.19 |
| 43 | 2.86 | 269.03 | 33.01 |
| 44 | 2.97 | 280.91 | 32.83 |
| 45 | 3.09 | 293.26 | 32.64 |
| 46 | 3.21 | 306.12 | 32.45 |
| 47 | 3.34 | 319.48 | 32.25 |
| 48 | 3.47 | 333.38 | 32.05 |
| 49 | 3.61 | 347.83 | 31.85 |
| 50 | 3.76 | 362.87 | 31.64 |
| 51 | 3.91 | | |

## Question 17.6

a) This can be looked at as a call option on the 1m shares with strike price $K = 50m$ with an infinite time to expiration (it pays no dividends). The price of the land should be worth $100m; the reason for this is the PV of the excavation cost $[PV(K)]$ is zero, for we should never exercise it early. Say the land was worth $75m. We could short 1 million shares (receive $100m), buy the land and put the $25m in the risk-free asset. Eventually that $25m will grow to over $50m, and the buried shares will be able to cover our short sale.

b) By similar reasoning, let the land be worth $C$ and suppose we do the same exercise except this time we cover our short sale by digging up the shares just before the dividend gets paid. In 10 years, we will have a cash flow (in $ millions), $(100 - C)\, e^{0.05(10)} - 50$. This must be equal to zero, i.e., the land is worth

$$C = 100 - 50e^{-0.5} = 69.673. \tag{17}$$

c) This can now be treated as a perpetual American call on the stock with dividend yield 1 percent; it will have a value of 75.26 and should get exercised at $S = 500$.

## Question 17.8

a) Each period, the expected price of a widget is $0.25/2 + 2.25/2 = \$1.25$.

b) The expected cash flow each period is

$$\frac{0.25 - 1}{2} + \frac{2.25 - 1}{2} = 0.25 \tag{18}$$

which will have an NPV of $0.25/0.05 - 10 = -5$. It will never be optimal to produce.

c) If we can only produce when the widget price is 2.25, we can have expected cash flows of $1.25/2 = 0.625$ (i.e., the second term in the above equation). This will yield an $NPV = 0.625/0.05 - 10 = 2.5$.

d) If the widget price is either $0.10 or $2.40 with equal probability, then the expected widget price remains $1.25, but expected cash flow is $0.50 (0) + 0.50(\$2.50 - \$1) = \$0.75$, which increases our NPV to 5. Note that if the variance of the widget price is greater, expected cash flow is greater. In effect, producing only when it is profitable amounts to having a call option each period, with the strike price being the marginal cost of production. Increases in volatility raise the value of this call.

## Question 17.10

a) We have to calculate the discount rate using the CAPM.

We have: $\alpha = 0.06 - 0.50 \times (0.10 - 0.06) = 0.04$

The expected cash flow is:

$$E(X) = 0.6 \times 50 + 0.4 \times 100 = 70.$$

We can calculate $V$, which is the value of the project as

$$V = \frac{E(X)}{(1+\alpha)^T} = \frac{70}{(1+0.04)^1} = 67.3077.$$

b) In order to calculate the risk-neutral probability, we need

$$F_{0,1} = 67.3077 \times 1.06 = 71.3462.$$

The risk-neutral probability is:

$$p^* = \frac{F_{0,T} - X_d}{X_u - X_d} = \frac{71.3462 - 100}{50 - 100} = 0.573.$$

Hence, we can use the formula to evaluate:

$$V = \frac{0.5731 \times 50 + (1 - 0.5731) \times 100}{1.06} = 67.307$$

## Question 17.12

The discount rate is $r + \beta(r_m - r) = 0.05 + 0.5(0.08) = 0.09$. The current value of the future cash flows will be $8/0.09 = 88.889$. The static NPV is negative at $88.89 - 100 = -11.11$. Using the binomial model, we need a dividend yield. As in the widget problem, the dividend yield will be the cash flow divided by the PV of the cash flows, which is just the discount rate 0.09. For our options analysis, we must use $r = \ln(1.05)$ and $\delta = \ln(1.04)$. Using a three-step forward tree (see Table Two on the next page), we see we would invest in the project in two years in the up-up node; this gives a value of 12.45. With over 100 steps the project has a value around 12.34. With perpetual investment rights, we could use the perpetual call real option

$$\text{CallPerpetual}(8/0.09, 100, 0.35, \ln(1.05), \ln(1.09)) = \{19.64, 199.28\}. \tag{21}$$

The project is worth 19.64; the right to invest after three years adds approximately 50 percent to the project value.

### Table Two (Problem 17.12)

| Time (yrs) | 1 | 2 | 3 |
|---|---|---|---|
| | | | 227.0623 |
| | | | 127.0623 |
| | | 166.1037 | |
| | | **66.10367** | |
| | 121.510371 | | 112.7558 |
| | 28.8305216 | | 12.75582 |
| PV(CF)  88.88889 | | 82.48464 | |
| V of Proj.  12.45509 | | 5.021933 | |
| | 60.3402646 | | 55.99288 |
| | 1.97712275 | | 0 |
| | | 40.96066 | |
| | | 0 | |
| | | | 27.80524 |
| | | | 0 |

American Call
Strike = 100
Vol = 35.00%; r = 4.88%
Exp = 3 years; Div = 8.62%
u = 1.367; d = 0.679
Risk-neutral prob of up = 0.413
Forward tree

## Question 17.14

The residual value of the land effectively lowers the extraction costs (i.e., the strike price) by $R = 1$. We must now solve as in the examples:

$$S_t = \frac{\ln(1.05)}{\ln(1.04)} 12.60 = 15.674. \tag{25}$$

It will take $t$ years where $15\,(1.009615)^t = 15.674$ for a solution of $t = 4.5932$. The value of the land is the NPV, which will be

$$\frac{15.674 - 12.60}{1.05^{4.5932}} = 2.4568. \tag{26}$$

This is higher than extracting now, which would give us 2.40. Note the NPV (as of today) for extracting in $T$ years is

$$\frac{1}{1.05^T}\left(15\frac{1.05^T}{1.04^T} - 13.60 + 1\right) = \frac{15}{1.04^T} - \frac{12.60}{1.05^T}, \tag{27}$$

and we could maximize this directly.

## Question 17.16

If shutdown and startup were costless, we would only produce if $S > 8$, and we would shut down if $S < 8$; hence, $S_* = S^* = 8$. If there is no cost of undoing options, there will be no hysteresis (e.g., producers will never be producing at a loss).

## Question 17.18

As in Example 17.1, we receive an underlying cash flow worth $300/0.03 = 10,000$ by paying a strike of the mine cost plus the PV of the cost of extraction $250/0.05 + 1,000 = 6000$. Note the dividend implied by the lease rate is $10,000\,(0.03) = 300$ and equal to the interest cost on the strike $6,000(0.05) = 300$. This implies that there is no value to waiting. Using the call option method,

$$\text{CallPerpetual}\,(10000, 6000, 0.0001, \ln(1.05), \ln(1.03)) = \{4000, 9903.68\}. \tag{33}$$

The mine is worth its current NPV.

## Question 17.20

The value of a producing mine is

$$V_p(S) = \frac{S}{0.03} - 5{,}000 + \text{PutPerpetual}\left(\frac{S}{0.03}, \frac{250}{0.05}, 0.2, \ln(1.05), \ln(1.03)\right), \qquad (36)$$

which is the value of not shutting down the mine plus the value of being able to shutdown. Working backwards, if $\overline{S}$ is the trigger price of our mine investment [i.e., we receive $V_p\left(\overline{S}\right)$ when $S_t = \overline{S}$ ], the current value is

$$V(S,\ \overline{S}) = \left(\frac{300}{\overline{S}}\right)^{h_1} \times \left(V_p\left(\overline{S}\right) - 1000\right). \qquad (37)$$

Using $h_1 = 1.5812$, we want to choose $\overline{S}$ to maximize the above quantity. Using Excel's solver or other numerical program $\overline{S} = 464.00$ and $V(300, \overline{S}) = 4{,}830.21$. Note the trigger price is lower than when there is no shutdown option.

# Chapter 18

## The Lognormal Distribution

### Question 18.2

If $z$ is standard normal, $\mu + \sigma \times z$ is $N\left(\mu, \sigma^2\right)$. The five draws from a standard normal distribution can therefore be transformed as: $0.8 + 5\,(-1.7) = -7.7$, $0.8 + 5\,(0.55) = 3.55$, $0.8 + 5\,(-0.3) = -0.7$, $0.8 + 5\,(-0.02) = 0.7$, and $0.8 + 5\,(0.85) = 5.05$.

### Question 18.4

Sums and differences of two random variables are normally distributed; hence, $x_1 + x_2$ is normally distributed with mean $\mu_1 + \mu_2 = 10$ and variance

$$\sigma_1^2 + \sigma_2^2 + 2\rho\sigma_1\sigma_2 = 0.5 + 14 + \left[2 \times (-0.3) \times \sqrt{0.5 \times 14}\right] = 10.3.$$

The difference is normally distributed with mean $\mu_1 - \mu_2 = -6$ and (higher) variance

$$\sigma_1^2 + \sigma_2^2 - 2\rho\sigma_1\sigma_2 = 0.5 + 14 + \left[2 \times (-0.3) \times \sqrt{0.5 \times 14}\right] = 18.7.$$

### Question 18.6

If $x \sim N\left(\mu, \sigma^2\right)$ then $E\,(e^x) = e^{\mu + 0.5\sigma}$; using the given numbers, $E\,(e^x) = e^{2+2.5} = 90.017$. There is a 50 percent probability $x$ is below its mean of 2; hence, the median of $e^x$ is $e^2 = 7.3891$.

### Question 18.8

Since $S_t = S_0 \exp\left[\left(\alpha - \tfrac{1}{2}\sigma^2\right)t + \sigma\sqrt{t}\,z\right]$ where $z$ is standard normal,

$$P\left(S_t > 105\right) = P\left[\left(\alpha - \frac{1}{2}\sigma^2\right)t + \sigma\sqrt{t}\,z > \ln\left(\frac{105}{100}\right)\right]$$

$$= P\left(z > \frac{\ln\left(\frac{105}{100}\right) - \left(\alpha - \tfrac{1}{2}\sigma^2\right)t}{\sigma\sqrt{t}}\right)$$

$$= P\left(z < \frac{-\ln\left(\frac{105}{100}\right) + \left(\alpha - \tfrac{1}{2}\sigma^2\right)t}{\sigma\sqrt{t}}\right) = N\,(d_2)$$

where $d_2 = \left[\ln(100/105) + \left(\alpha - \frac{1}{2}\sigma^2\right)t\right]/\left(\sigma\sqrt{t}\right)$. Using the given parameters, $d_2 = 0.045967$ and $N(d_2) = 0.4817$. For this parameter specification, the probability $S_t > 105$ increases with $t$ and decreases with $\sigma$. Analytically, since $N'(d_2) > 0$, the derivative will have the same sign as $\partial d_2/\partial t$ and $\partial d_2/\partial \sigma$. Specifically,

$$\frac{\partial P(S_t > K)}{\partial t} = N'(d_2)\frac{\left(\alpha - \sigma^2/2\right) - \ln(S_0/K)/t}{2\sigma^2\sqrt{t}} > 0$$

since $\alpha - \sigma^2/2 = 0.035 > 0$ and $\ln(S_0/K) < 0$. As an example, if $t$ is five years, there there is a 57.46 percent chance of being greater than 105. For volatility, let $t = 1$. Then

$$\frac{\partial P(S_t > K)}{\partial \sigma} = -N'(d_2)\left(\frac{\alpha - \ln(S_0/K)}{2\sigma^2} + \frac{1}{4}\right) > 0$$

## Question 18.10

We have

$$P(S_t < 98) = P\left[\left(\alpha - \frac{1}{2}\sigma^2\right)t + \sigma\sqrt{t}z < \ln\left(\frac{98}{100}\right)\right]$$

$$= P\left(z < \frac{-\ln\left(\frac{98}{100}\right) + \left(\alpha - \frac{1}{2}\sigma^2\right)t}{\sigma\sqrt{t}}\right) = N(-d_2)$$

with $-d_2 = (\ln(98/100) - 0.035)/0.3 = -0.18401$. Hence $P(S_t < 98) = N(-0.18401) = 42.70\%$.

## Question 18.12

See Figure Two on the next page. Option prices depend on the conditional (risk neutral) expectation, not the probability that the option is in the money. As $T$ increases, so does the likelihood that $S_T > K_T$ may be lower; however, the payoff depends on the conditional expectation (since the option does not pay a constant amount). The increased dispersion offsets the lower probability (for the call option).

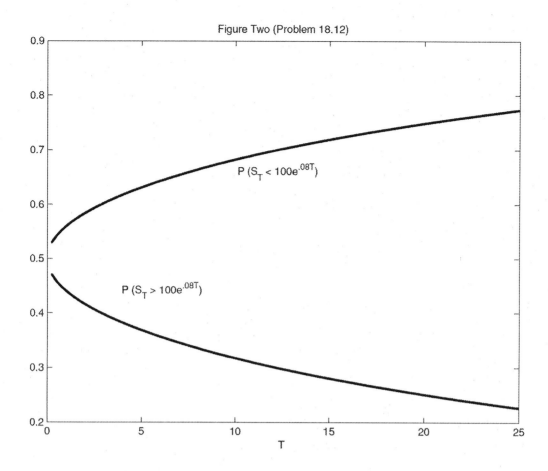

Figure Two (Problem 18.12)

## Question 18.14

The mean should be varying year by year whereas the standard deviation should be more stable.

# Chapter 19

## Monte Carlo Valuation

### Question 19.2

The histogram should be similar to a standard normal density ("bell" shaped). Since a uniform distribution has a mean of 0.5 and a variance of 1/12, the mean of $\sum_{i=1}^{12} u_i - 6$ is zero and the variance (and standard deviation) will be 1 since

$$\text{var}\left(\sum_{i=1}^{12} u_i\right) = 12\,\text{var}(u_i) = 1.$$

### Question 19.4

The standard deviation of the estimate will be $s_n/n$ where $s_n$ is the sample standard deviation of the $n$ simulations. Since $s_n$ is close to 2.9, $n = 84{,}000$ should give a standard error close to 0.01.

### Question 19.6

The simulations should be generated by $S_1 = 100\exp\left(0.06 + 0.4^2/2 + 0.4z\right)$ where $z$ is standard normal. The claim prices should be $e^{-0.06}\,\overline{S^\alpha}$ where $\alpha$ is the relevant power and the $\overline{S^\alpha}$ is the average from the simulations. These values should be close to

$$100^\alpha \exp\left[(\alpha - 1)\left(0.06 + \frac{\alpha}{2}0.4^2\right)\right].$$

Using this, the three values should be close to 12,461, 9.51, and 0.000135 respectively.

## Question 19.8

By log normality

$$P(S_t < 95) = P\left\{100 \exp\left[\left(0.1 - 0.2^2/2\right)t + 0.2\sqrt{t}z\right] < 95\right\}$$

$$P\left(z < \frac{\ln(95/100) - \left(0.1 - 0.2^2/2\right)t}{0.2\sqrt{t}}\right)$$

with $t = 1/365$, this is $N(-4.9207) = 4 \times 10^{-7}$. This magnitude negative return should, on average, occur once every 2.5 million days. With $t = 1/252$ (i.e., one trading day) this becomes $N(-4.0965) = 2.097 \times 10^{-5}$; making such a drop is similarly unlikely.

## Question 19.10

The simulations should be done by generating 1,000 standard normals $\varepsilon_1$ and another 1,000 (independent) standard normals $\varepsilon_2$. Then let $S_1 = 40 \exp\left(\frac{0.08 - 0.3/2}{12} + \frac{0.3}{\sqrt{12}}\varepsilon_1\right)$ and let $S_2 = 100 \exp\left(\frac{0.08 - 0.5/2}{12} + \frac{0.5}{\sqrt{12}}z\right)$ where $z = 0.45\varepsilon_1 + \sqrt{1 - 0.45^2}\varepsilon_2$. The means, standard deviations, and correlation from Monte Carlo should approximate their theoretical counterparts.

## Question 19.12

See Table One for a typical simulation. With weekly data, the lognormality (as opposed to normal) of the stock price isn't strong (i.e., there is little skewness or kurtosis). This implies the simple return is not that different from the continuous (normal) return. However, when we look at yearly distributions, there is now significant kurtosis and skewness.

TABLE ONE (Problem 19.12)

|          | Returns Week | Returns Year | Stock Price Week | Stock Price Year |
|----------|--------|--------|----------|----------|
| Mean     | 0.0030 | 0.1551 | 100.3862 | 122.1316 |
| SD       | 0.0415 | 0.2995 | 4.1708   | 37.4255  |
| Skewness | 0.0013 | 0.0013 | 0.1267   | 0.9511   |
| Kurtosis | 3.0133 | 3.0133 | 3.0390   | 4.6230   |

## Question 19.14

Using simple gross returns (i.e., *Payoff/Cost*), the mean should be around 1.62, the standard deviation around 1.49, skewness around 1.79, and kurtosis around 7.59.

## Question 19.16

We can write down the optimal exercise schedule based on our results in exercise 19.15.

| Path | $t=1$ | $t=2$ | $t=3$ |
|------|-------|-------|-------|
| 1 | 0 | 0 | 0 |
| 2 | 0 | 0 | 0 |
| 3 | 0 | 0 | 1 |
| 4 | 1 | 0 | 0 |
| 5 | 0 | 0 | 0 |
| 6 | 1 | 0 | 0 |
| 7 | 1 | 0 | 0 |
| 8 | 1 | 0 | 0 |

The cash flows associated with this exercise schedule are:

| Path | $t=1$ | $t=2$ | $t=3$ |
|------|-------|-------|-------|
| 1 | 0 | 0 | 0 |
| 2 | 0 | 0 | 0 |
| 3 | 0 | 0 | 0.07 |
| 4 | 0.17 | 0 | 0 |
| 5 | 0 | 0 | 0 |
| 6 | 0.34 | 0 | 0 |
| 7 | 0.18 | 0 | 0 |
| 8 | 0.22 | 0 | 0 |

At $t=0$, we therefore have the following continuation values

| pv (continuation) |
|-------------------|
| 0 |
| 0 |
| 0.058468915 |
| 0.160099971 |
| 0 |
| 0.320199941 |
| 0.169517616 |
| 0.207188197 |

At $t = 0$, we can just estimate a regression with a constant, because the stock price and the squared stock price are constant and equal to 1. All paths have an immediate exercise value of $1.1 - 1 = 0.1$, and thus need to be included in the regression. The coefficient on the constant of this regression is 0.114. This is larger than the intrinsic value of 0.1; therefore, early exercise is never optimal in $t = 0$.

Hence, we can find the value of the American put option to be:

| |
| --- |
| 0 |
| 0 |
| 0.058468915 |
| 0.160099971 |
| 0 |
| 0.320199941 |
| 0.169517616 |
| 0.207188197 |
| 0.11443433      = average(values above) |

For the European put option, we take the payoffs at $t = 3$, discount them at the risk-free rate, and then average the payoffs. We have:

| Discounted Payoff | Payoff $t = 3$ |
| --- | --- |
| 0 | 0 |
| 0 | 0 |
| 0.058468915 | 0.07 |
| 0.150348638 | 0.18 |
| 0 | 0 |
| 0.167054042 | 0.2 |
| 0.075174319 | 0.09 |
| 0 | 0 |
| 0.056380739 | = average() |

# Chapter 20

## Brownian Motion and Itô's Lemma

### Question 20.2

If $y = S_2$ then $S = \sqrt{y}$ and $dy = \left(2S\alpha(S,t) + \sigma(S,t)^2\right)dt + 2S\sigma(S,t)dZ_t$, where $\alpha$ $(S,\ t)$ is the drift of $S$ and $\sigma$ $(S,\ t)$ is the volatility of $S$. For the three specifications:

a) $dy = \left(2\alpha\sqrt{y} + \sigma^2\right)dt + 2\sqrt{y}\sigma dZ_t$.

b)

$$dy = \left(2\sqrt{y}\lambda\left(a - \sqrt{y}\right) + \sigma^2\right)dt + 2\sqrt{y}\sigma dZ_t \tag{1}$$

$$= \left(2\lambda a\sqrt{y} - 2\lambda y + \sigma^2\right)dt + 2\sqrt{y}\sigma dZ_t. \tag{2}$$

c) $dy = \left(2\alpha + \sigma^2\right)y\,dt + 2\sigma y\,dZ_t$.

### Question 20.4

If $y = \sqrt{S}$ then $S = y^2$ and

$$dy = \left(\frac{1}{2}S^{-1/2}\alpha(S,t) - \frac{1}{8}S^{-3/2}\sigma(S,t)^2\right)dt + \frac{1}{2}S^{-1/2}\sigma(S,t)dZ_t \tag{3}$$

$$= \left(\frac{1}{2y}\alpha(S,t) - \frac{1}{8y^3}\sigma(S,t)^2\right)dt + \frac{1}{2y}\sigma(S,t)dZ_t \tag{4}$$

a) $dy = \left(\frac{\alpha}{2y} - \frac{\sigma^2}{8y^3}\right)dt - \frac{\sigma}{2y}dZ_t$

b) $dy = \left(\frac{\lambda\alpha}{2y} - \frac{\lambda}{2y^2} - \frac{\sigma^2}{8y^3}\right)dt - \frac{\sigma}{2y}dZ_t$.

c) $dy = \left(\frac{\alpha}{2} - \frac{\sigma^2}{8}\right)y\,dt - \frac{\sigma}{2}dZ_t$.

## Question 20.6

If $y = \ln(SQ) = \ln(S) + \ln(Q)$ then

$$dy = d\ln(S) + d\ln(Q) \tag{6}$$

$$= \left(\alpha_S - \delta_S - \sigma_S^2/2 + \alpha_Q - \delta_Q - \sigma_Q^2/2\right)dt + \sigma_S dZ_S + \sigma_Q dZ_Q. \tag{7}$$

## Question 20.8

Since the process $y = S_a Q_b$ follows geometric Brownian motion (i.e., $dy = \alpha_y\, y\, d t + \sigma_y\, y\, d Z_y$), the price of the claims will be $e^{-r}E^*(y_1) = y_0 e^{(\alpha_y - r)}$. We use Ito's lemma, as in equation (20.38), with $\delta = 0$ and $\alpha_S = \alpha_Q = r$ to arrive at the drift

$$\alpha_y = ar + br + \frac{1}{2}a(a-1)\sigma_S^2 + \frac{1}{2}b(b-1)\sigma_Q^2 + ab\rho\sigma_S\sigma_Q \tag{9}$$

$$= 0.06(a+b) + \frac{0.4^2}{2}a(a-1) + \frac{0.2^2}{2}b(b-1) - 0.3(0.4)(0.2)ab. \tag{10}$$

a) Since $a = b = 1$, $y_0 = 10{,}000$ and $\alpha_y = 0.12 - 0.024 = 0.096$; hence, the claim is worth $10{,}000e^{0.096-0.06} = 10{,}366.56$.

b) Since $a = 1$ and $b = -1$, $y_0 = 1$ and $\alpha_y = 0.2^2 + 0.024 = 0.064$ hence the claim is worth $e^{0.064-0.06} = 1.004$.

c) Since $a = 1/2$ and $b = 1/2$, $y_0 = 100$ and $\alpha_y = 0.029$; hence, the claim is worth $100e^{0.029-0.06} = 96.948$.

d) Since $a = -1$ and $b = -1$, $y_0 = 1/10{,}000$ and $\alpha_y = 0.056$; hence, the claim is worth $\left(e^{0.056-0.06}\right)/10{,}000 = 9.9601 \times 10^{-5}$.

e) Since $a = 2$ and $b = 1$, $y_0 = 1{,}000{,}000$ and $\alpha_y = 0.292$; hence, the claim is worth $1{,}000{,}000e^{0.292-0.06} = 1.2612$ million.

## Question 20.10

Note that if $V(S)$ satisfies the given equation, then

$$E^*(dV) = \left[(r-\delta)SV_S + \frac{1}{2}\sigma^2 S^2 V_{SS}\right]dt = rVdt. \tag{13}$$

Since $V(S) = kS^{h_1}$ where $a$ is constant, showing $y = S^a$ satisfies $E^*(dy) = rydt$ when $a = h_1$ is sufficient (i.e., the constant term is irrelevant). Using Ito's lemma,

$$E^*(dy) = aS^{a-1}(r-\delta)S + \frac{1}{2}a(a-1)S^{a-2}\sigma^2 S^2 \tag{14}$$

$$= \left( a(r-\delta)y + a(a-1)\frac{\sigma^2}{2}y \right)dt. \tag{15}$$

If $E^*(dy) = rydt$, then $a$ must satisfy

$$a(r-\delta) + a(a-1)\frac{\sigma^2}{2} = r. \tag{16}$$

The two solutions are $h_1$ and $h_2$ as given in the derivation of the perpetual call formula in Chapter 12. You can back them out using the square root formula.

## Question 20.12

Strategy: Buy $\dfrac{1}{\sigma_1 S_1}$ units of stock 1 and buy $\dfrac{1}{\sigma_2 S_2}$ units of stock 2. Finance the difference by borrowing at the risk-free interest rate. The return to the portfolio of the two assets and the borrowed amount is:

$$\frac{1}{\sigma_1 S_1}dS_1 + \frac{1}{\sigma_2 S_2}dS_2 + Irdt$$

$$= \frac{1}{\sigma_1 S_1}(\alpha_1 S_1 dt + \sigma_1 S_1 dZ) + \frac{1}{\sigma_2 S_2}(\alpha_2 S_2 dt - \sigma_2 S_2 dZ) + \left( -\frac{1}{\sigma_1 S_1}S_1 - \frac{1}{\sigma_2 S_2}S_2 \right)rdt$$

$$= \frac{\alpha_1}{\sigma_1}dt + dZ + \frac{\alpha_2}{\sigma_2}dt - dZ - \frac{r}{\sigma_1}dt - \frac{r}{\sigma_2}dt$$

$$= \left( \frac{\alpha_1 - r}{\sigma_1} + \frac{\alpha_2 - r}{\sigma_2} \right)dt$$

Because the portfolio is self-financing and riskless, its return should be zero to avoid arbitrage. We have indeed demonstrated that the Sharpe ratios sum to zero.

## Question 20.14

As mentioned in the problem, $\sigma d\, Z$ appears in both $dS$ and $dQ$. One can think of $dQ$ as an alternative model for the stock (with $dS$ being the standard geometric Brownian motion).

a) If there were no jumps, $dQ$ would also be geometric Brownian motion. Since it has the same risk component, $\sigma d\, Z$, $\alpha_Q$ must equal $\alpha$. If we thought of $Q$ as another traded asset, this naturally follows from no arbitrage.

b) If $Y_1 > 1$, then there are only positive jumps. We would, therefore, expect $\alpha_Q < \alpha$ to compensate for this. Mathematically, $d\, Q/Q - dS/S = (\alpha_Q - \alpha)\, dt + dq_1$. If a jump occurs, $dq_1 = Y_1 - 1 > 0$; if $\alpha_Q \geq \alpha$, we could buy $Q$ and short $S$. The only risk we have is jump risk, but this will always be "good" news for our portfolio. In order to avoid this arbitrage, $\alpha_Q$ must be less than $\alpha$.

If we use a weaker assumption $k_1 = E\, (Y_1 - 1) > 0$ and we assume the returns to $S$ and $Q$ should be the same (this makes sense if we are looking at $Q$ as an alternative model instead of another stock), then we arrive at a similar result. The expected return to $Q$ is $\alpha_Q + \lambda_1 k_1$; setting this equal to $\alpha$ implies $\alpha - \alpha_Q = \lambda_1 k_1 > 0$.

c) Let $\alpha^*$ be the expected return of $Q$. Note that $\alpha_Q$ is not the expected return; it is the expected return conditional on no jumps occurring. We have the following relationship,

$$\alpha^* = E\left(\frac{dQ}{Q}\right) / dt = \alpha_Q + k_1\lambda_1 + k_2\lambda_2 \tag{32}$$

where $k_i = E\, (Y_i - 1)$. Hence $\alpha_Q = \alpha^* - k_1\lambda_1 - k_2\lambda_2$. If $\alpha^* = \alpha$ (i.e., $Q$ and $S$ have the same expected return) then $\alpha - \alpha_Q = k_1\lambda_1 + k_2\lambda_2$. The sign of which could be positive or negative if there are no restriction on $k_1$ and $k_2$.

# Chapter 21

## The Black-Scholes-Merton Equation

### Question 21.2

If $V(S, t) = AS^a e^{\gamma t}$, then $V_t = \gamma V$, $V_S = aAS^{a-1}e^{\gamma t} = aV/S$, and $V_{SS} = a(a-1)AS^{a-2}e^{\gamma t} = a(a-1)V/S^2$. Therefore, the left hand side of the Black-Scholes equation (21.11) is

$$V_t + (r-\delta)V_S S + V_{SS}S^2\sigma^2/2 - rV = \left(\gamma - r + (r-\delta)a + \frac{\sigma^2}{2}a(a-1)\right)V. \tag{1}$$

We can rewrite the coefficient of $V$ as

$$\gamma + (r-\delta)a + \frac{\sigma^2}{2}a(a-1) = \frac{\sigma^2}{2}a^2 + \left(r - \delta - \frac{\sigma^2}{2}\right)a + \gamma - r. \tag{2}$$

From the quadratic formula, this has roots

$$a = \frac{-\left(r-\delta-\frac{\sigma^2}{2}\right)}{\sigma^2} \pm \frac{\sqrt{\left(r-\delta-\frac{\sigma^2}{2}\right)^2 - 4\frac{\sigma^2}{2}(\gamma-r)}}{\sigma^2}. \tag{3}$$

Simplifying,

$$a = \left(\frac{1}{2} - \frac{r-\delta}{\sigma^2}\right) \pm \sqrt{\left(\frac{r-\delta}{\sigma^2} - \frac{1}{2}\right)^2 + \frac{2(r-\gamma)}{\sigma^2}}. \tag{4}$$

Note, for a given $\gamma$, these are the only values for $a$ that will satisfy the PDE.

### Question 21.4

Defining $V(S, t) = Ke^{-r(T-t)} + Se^{-\delta(T-t)}$, we have $V_t = rKe^{-r(T-t)} + \delta Se^{-\delta(T-t)}$, $V_S = e^{-\delta(T-t)}$, and $V_{SS} = 0$. The Black-Scholes equation is satisfied for $V_t + (r-\delta)V_S S + V_{SS}S^2\sigma^2/2$

$$rKe^{-r(T-t)} + \delta Se^{-\delta(T-t)} + (r-\delta)e^{-\delta(T-t)}S \tag{10}$$

$$= r\left(Ke^{-r(T-t)} + Se^{-\delta(T-t)}\right) = rV. \tag{11}$$

This also follows from the result that linear combinations of solutions of the PDE are also solutions. The boundary condition is $V(S, T) = K + S_T$ (i.e., we receive one share and $K$ dollars). Similarly, a long forward contract with value $Se^{-\delta(T-t)} - Ke^{-r(T-t)}$ will solve the PDE.

## Question 21.6

Let $V(S, t) = e^{-r(T-t)}N(d_2)$; we must show $V$ solves the PDE $V_t + (r - \delta) SV_S + S^2\sigma^2 V_{SS}/2 = rV$. Note that

$$d_2 = \frac{\ln(S/K)}{\sigma\sqrt{T-t}} + \left(\frac{r - \delta - \sigma^2/2}{\sigma}\right)\sqrt{T-t} \tag{17}$$

depends on both $S$ and $t$. Beginning with the first term in the PDE,

$$V_t = rV + e^{-r(T-t)}N'(d_2)\left(\frac{\ln(S/K)}{2\sigma(T-t)^{3/2}} - \frac{r - \delta - \sigma^2/2}{2\sigma(T-t)^{1/2}}\right)$$

$$= rV + \frac{e^{-r(T-t)}N'(d_2)}{2(T-t)}\left(d_2 - \frac{2(r - \delta - \sigma^2/2)}{\sigma}\sqrt{T-t}\right). \tag{18}$$

Since $V_S = e^{-r(T-t)}N'(d_2)\big/\left(S\sigma\sqrt{T-t}\right)$ the second term in the PDE is

$$(r - \delta)SV_S = \left(\frac{r - \delta}{\sigma\sqrt{T-t}}\right)e^{-r(T-t)}N'(d_2). \tag{19}$$

The second partial of $V$ with respect to $S$ is

$$V_{SS} = \frac{e^{-r(T-t)}\left(N''(d_2) - N'(d_2)\right)}{S^2\sigma^2(T-t)} = -\frac{e^{-r(T-t)}N'(d_2)}{S^2\sigma^2(T-t)}\left(d_2 + \sigma\sqrt{T-t}\right) \tag{20}$$

where we use the property $N(x) = -xN(x)$. The third term in the PDE is, therefore,

$$\frac{S^2\sigma^2 V_{SS}}{2} = -\frac{e^{-r(T-t)}N'(d_2)}{2(T-t)}\left(d_2 + \sigma\sqrt{T-t}\right). \tag{21}$$

Adding equations (18), (19), and (21), all terms cancel expect the $rV$ term in equation (18) (i.e., $V$ satisfies the PDE).

## Question 21.8

These bets are all or nothing options. The cash bets being worth, per dollar, $e^{-rT}N(d_2)$ if we receive $1 if $S_T > K$ and worth $e^{-rT}N(-d_2)$ if we receive $1 if $S_T < K$. The stock bets being worth, per share, $SN(d_1)$ if we receive 1 share if $S_T > K$ and worth $SN(-d_1)$ if we receive 1 share if $S_T < K$. (Note we are assuming the current time is $t = 0$ and the bet is for the stock price $T$ years from now).

a)  By setting $K = Se^{(r-\delta)T}, d_2 = -\sigma\sqrt{T}/2$ the value of the bet that the share price will exceed the forward price is $e^{-rT}N\left(-\sigma\sqrt{T}/2\right)$. This is always less than the opposite bet, which has value $e^{-rT}N\left(\sigma\sqrt{T}/2\right)$.

b)  If denominated in cash, we could make the bet fair by setting the strike price equal to $K = Se^{(r-\delta-0.5\sigma^2)T}$, which is the median (i.e., 50 percent of the probability is above this value). This will make $d_2 = 0$ and the bets worth $e^{-rT}/2$, which is not a surprise since the sum of the two bets must be worth $e^{-rT}$. Using $T = 1$, $r = 6\%$, $\sigma = 30\%$, we have $K = 100e^{0.06-0.3^2/2} = 101.51$.

c)  If denominated in shares, we could make the bet fair by setting the strike price equal to $K = Se^{(r-\delta+0.5\sigma^2)T} = 100e^{0.06+0.3^2/2} = 111.07$, which is above the forward price. This makes $d_1 = 0$ and the bets worth $S/2 = 50$.

## Question 21.10

If we purchase one unit of the claim, $-V_S$ shares, and invest $W$ in the risk free bond, our investment is worth $I = V(S, t) - V_S S + W = 0$. By purchasing one claim, we will receive a dividend of $\Gamma d$ that will be added to $dI$. The change in the investment value is

$$dI = \Gamma dt + V_t dt + V_S dS + \frac{\sigma^2 S^2 V_{SS} dt}{2} - V_S dS - V_S \delta S dt + rW dt \tag{25}$$

$$= \left(\Gamma + V_t + \tfrac{1}{2}\sigma^2 S^2 V_{SS} - V_S \delta S + rW\right) dt. \tag{26}$$

Since this is risk free and is (initially) a zero investment, both the drift and $I$ must be zero. This

$$\Gamma + V_t + \tfrac{1}{2}\sigma^2 S^2 V_{SS} - V_S \delta S + r\left(V_S S - V\right) = 0; \tag{27}$$

hence,

$$\Gamma + V_t + \tfrac{1}{2}\sigma^2 S^2 V_{SS} + \left(r - \delta\right) V_S S = rV. \tag{28}$$

Note that if we assume $\Gamma$ is a continuous yield of the claim (rather than a \$ per unit rate), the first term would be $\Gamma V$ rather than $\Gamma$.

## Question 21.12

Setting $b = -1$ and using Proposition 21.1, we change the dividend yield of $S$ to $\eta = 0.02 - 0.2$ $(0.3)(0.5) = -0.01$. The prepaid forward price, i.e., $V$ in equation (21.35), is $S_0 e^{-\eta T}$. Letting $\delta^* = 0.06 + (0.06 - 0.01) - 0.5^2 = -0.14$, we have the value of the claim being

$$\frac{1}{90} e^{0.2(2)} \left( 50 e^{0.01(2)} \right) = 0.8455.$$ (32)

Using Proposition 20.4, the claim should be worth

$$S_0 e^{-\delta T} \left( Q_0^b e^{\left( b(r-\delta_Q) + 0.5b(b-1)\sigma_Q^2 \right)2} \right) e^{b\rho\sigma\sigma_Q T},$$ (33)

which equals

$$50 e^{-0.04} \left( 90^{-1} e^{\left( -0.05 + 0.5^2 \right)2} \right) e^{0.03(2)} = 0.8455.$$ (34)

Note that Proposition 20.4 derives the forward price; upon discounting, the forward price of $S$ becomes $S_0 e^{-\delta T}$ and the forward price of $Q_b$ term does not get discounted.

## Question 21.14

Using Proposition 21.1, since $b = 1$, the insurance payoff should be worth

$$Q e^{(r-\delta_Q)T} V(S, K, \sigma_S, r, T, \delta - \rho\sigma \sigma_S);$$ (37)

hence, we should use a dividend yield of $0.02 + 0.2(0.3)(0.5) = 0.05$, making the put relatively more valuable. For $K = 50$, $V = 7.09$; hence, the insurance is worth $90 e^{(0.06-0.01)2} (7.09) = 705.21$. If we wanted to insure $90 e^{(0.06-0.01)2} = 99.465$ units, it would cost $90 e^{(0.06-0.01)2} (6.05) = 601.77$. This is intuitive since $\ln(S)$ and $\ln(Q)$ are negatively correlated. When $Q$ is high, $S$ is more likely to be low, making the insurance payout larger (the holder has the right to sell *more* units for $K$).

# Chapter 22

## Risk-Neutral and Martingale Pricing

**Question 22.2**

We will evaluate a claim paying K if $S_T < K$.

Rewrite the condition for the payoff as $S_T < K \times P_T(T,T)$.

We can write the payoff of the claim as:

$$V(S_T,T) = K \times P_T(T,T) \times 1\big[S_T < K \times P_T(T,T)\big].$$

Using the stochastic discount factor to value the claim, we find that

$$V(S_0,0) = K \times P_0(0,T) \times E_0\left[\frac{U'(T)}{U'(0)} \times \frac{P_T(T,T)}{P_0(0,T)}\right] \times 1\big[S_T < K \times P_T(T,T)\big]$$

$$V(S_0,0) = K \times P_0(0,T) \times E_0^{P(T)}\Big[1\big[S_T < K \times P_T(T,T)\big]\Big].$$

Following 22.31, this is equal to

$$V(S_0,0) = K \times P_0(0,T) \times Pr^{P(T)}\left[\frac{S_T}{P_T(T,T)} < K\right].$$

Assuming that the price ratio follows a Brownian motion with constant volatility, we have that

$$\ln\left[\frac{S_T}{P_T(T,T)}\right] = \ln\left[\frac{S_t}{P_t(t,T)}\right] - 0.5\sigma^2(T-t) + \sigma z\sqrt{(T-t)}$$

$$V(S_0,0) = K \times P_0(0,T) \times Pr^{P(T)}\left[\ln\left[\frac{S_t}{P_t(t,T)}\right] - 0.5\sigma^2(T-t) + \sigma z\sqrt{(T-t)} < \ln(K)\right].$$

With $P_0(0,T) = e^{-rT}$ and $P_t(t,T) = e^{-r(T-t)}$, we have

$$V(S_0,0) = K \times e^{-rT} \times Pr^{P(T)}\left[z < \frac{\ln(K) - \ln(S_t) - (r - 0.5\sigma^2)(T-t)}{\sigma\sqrt{(T-t)}}\right]$$

$$V(S_0,0) = K \times e^{-rT} \times N\left[\frac{\ln(K) - \ln(S_t) - (r - 0.5\sigma^2)(T-t)}{\sigma\sqrt{(T-t)}}\right]$$

$$V(S_0,0) = K \times e^{-rT} \times N[-d_2],$$

which was to be shown.

## Question 22.4

We will evaluate a claim paying $S_1(T)$ if $S_1(T) > KS_2(T)$.

We can write the payoff of the claim as:

$$W(S_1(T), T) = S_1(T) \times 1\left[S_1(T) > K \times S_2(T)\right].$$

Using the stochastic discount factor to value the claim, we find that

$$W(S_1(t), t) = S_1(t) \times E_t\left[\frac{U'(T)}{U'(t)} \times \frac{S_1(T)}{S_1(t)}\right] \times 1\left[S_1(T) > K \times S_2(T)\right]$$

$$W(S_1(t), t) = S_1(t) \times E_t^{S_1}\left[1\left[S_1(T) > K \times S_2(T)\right]\right]$$

$$W(S_1(t), t) = S_1(t) \times E_t^{S_1}\left[1\left[\frac{1}{K} > \frac{S_2(T)}{S_1(T)}\right]\right]$$

$$W(S_1(t), t) = S_1(t) \times Pr^{S_1}\left[\frac{1}{K} > \frac{S_2(T)}{S_1(T)}\right].$$

Assuming that the ratio is a martingale with a constant standard deviation under the $S_1(t)$ measure, we have

$$d\left[\frac{S_2(t)}{S_1(t)}\right] \times \frac{S_1(t)}{S_2(t)} = \sigma dZ.$$

Where the standard derivation is calculated as (see Example 20.5 in the main textbook):

$$\sigma^2 = \sigma_1^2 + \sigma_2^2 - 2\rho\sigma_1\sigma_2.$$

Taking the natural log of the price ratio and using Itô's Lemma, we have

$$d\ln\left[\frac{S_2(t)}{S_1(t)}\right] = -0.5\sigma^2 dt + \sigma dZ.$$

We have with this process:

$$\ln\left[\frac{S_2(T)}{S_1(T)}\right] = \ln\left[\frac{S_2(t)}{S_1(t)}\right] - 0.5\sigma^2(T-t) + \sigma z\sqrt{T-t}.$$

So that

$$W(S_1(t), t) = S_1(t) \times Pr^{S_1}\left[\ln\frac{1}{K} > \ln\left[\frac{S_2(t)}{S_1(t)}\right] - 0.5\sigma^2(T-t) + \sigma z\sqrt{T-t}\right]$$

$$W(S_1(t), t) = S_1(t) \times Pr^{S_1}\left[z \leq \frac{\ln 1 - \ln K - \ln\left[S_2(t)\right] + \ln\left[S_1(t)\right] + 0.5\sigma^2(T-t)}{\sigma\sqrt{T-t}}\right]$$

$$W\left(S_1(t),t\right)=S_1(t)\times Pr^{S_1}\left[z\leq\frac{\ln\left[\frac{S_1(t)}{KS_2(t)}\right]+0.5\sigma^2\left(T-t\right)}{\sigma\sqrt{T-t}}\right].$$

Page 665 of the main textbook discusses that to derive the price with dividends, it suffices to consider the above formula as the prepaid forward price. We arrive at the price in terms of the stock price by replacing the price $S_i(t)$ with $S_i(t)\times e^{-\delta_i(T-t)}$.

$$W\left(S_1(t),t\right)=S_1(t)e^{-\delta_1(T-t)}\times Pr^{S_1}\left[z\leq\frac{\ln\left[\frac{S_1(t)e^{-\delta_1(T-t)}}{KS_2(t)e^{-\delta_2(T-t)}}\right]+0.5\sigma^2\left(T-t\right)}{\sigma\sqrt{T-t}}\right]$$

$$W\left(S_1(t),t\right)=S_1(t)e^{-\delta_1(T-t)}\times N\left[\frac{\ln\left[\frac{S_1(t)}{KS_2(t)}\right]+\left(\delta_2-\delta_1+0.5\sigma^2\right)\left(T-t\right)}{\sigma\sqrt{T-t}}\right],$$

which was to be shown.

## Question 22.6

You need to follow the simulation strategies of chapter 19 (Monte Carlo). Simulate

$$\left[\frac{S(T)}{P_T(T,T)}\right]=\frac{S_0}{P_0(0,T)}\exp\left(-0.5\sigma^2\left(T\right)+\sigma z\sqrt{T}\right)$$

and then calculate the price of the claim accordingly. You should find that it is very close to the theoretical value of $0.5766.

The mean of $x_T-x_0=\sigma x_0\sqrt{T}Z_T$ should be very close to zero and its standard deviation close to the value of $\sigma x_0\sqrt{T}=0.3\times\dfrac{41}{0.9802}\times\sqrt{0.25}=6.274$.

## Question 22.8

You need to follow the simulation strategies of Chapter 19 (Monte Carlo), in particular "simulating jumps with the Poisson distribution."

Calculate the price of the claim accordingly. You should find that it is very close to the theoretical value of $0.5865.

The mean of $x_T-x_0$ should be very close to zero and its standard deviation close to the theoretical value.

## Question 22.10

For the first part of the exercise, we model:

$$S_1(1) = S_1(0)\exp\left(0.06 - 0.05 - 0.50 \times .35^2(1) + 0.35z\sqrt{1}\right) \text{ and}$$

$$S_2(1) = S_2(0)\exp\left(0.06 - 0.12 - 0.50 \times .25^2(1) + 0.25w\sqrt{1}\right) \text{ where}$$

$$z = \varepsilon_1 \text{ and}$$

$$w = \rho\varepsilon_1 + \varepsilon_2\sqrt{1-\rho^2},$$

which uses the hint given in the exercise.

Don't forget to discount the payoff by the risk-free rate. Then you should get a value very close to the value given in the exercise, which is 15.850.

For the second part of the exercise, we model:

$$\frac{S_1(1)}{S_2(1)} = \frac{S_1(0)e^{-0.05}}{S_2(0)e^{-0.12}}\exp\left(-0.50 \times 0.3391^2(1) + 0.3391z\sqrt{1}\right)$$

where the standard deviation is calculated as:

$$\sigma^2 = \sigma_2^2 + \sigma_1^2 - 2\rho\sigma_1\sigma_2 = 0.35^2 + 0.25^2 - 2 \times 0.40 \times 0.35 \times 0.25$$

Note that you will have to take the dividend into account as well by replacing $S_2(0)$ with $S_2(0)e^{-0.12}$.

We get a value for the payoff that is very close to the value given in the exercise.

## Question 22.12

a)  You should find that the simulated drift per unit time is very close to –0.002.

b)  The fact that $r(1)$ is not a martingale complicates valuation. You will encounter, in Chapter 25, a model that can deal with this and derives a tractable solution.

## Question 22.14

This is not correct, and a similar argument to the one provided for the PBGC applies. Social security is currently underfunded; hence, your taxes pay for current retirees. Suppose social security tax proceeds were invested in the stock market. When do stock markets decrease or fall? They fall in difficult economic times. But these are the same situations in which tax revenues decrease because unemployment increases and people make less money. At the same time, the liabilities—paying monthly annuities after retirement—do not decrease proportionally; they stay flat or may even increase because some workers will be forced into early retirement. Hence, when the government needs the money most and marginal utility would be highest, the stock market investments cannot provide it.

# Chapter 23

## Exotic Options: II

### Question 23.2

In the same way as the COD, the paylater is priced initially using

$$0 = BSPut\ (S_0,\ K,\ \sigma,\ r,T\ ,\ \delta) - P \times DR(S_0,\ K,\ \sigma,\ r,T\ ,\ \delta,\ H\ ).$$

Thus, the amount to be paid if the barrier is hit is

$$P = \frac{BSPut(S_0,K,\sigma,r,T,\delta)}{DR(S_0,K,\sigma,r,T,\delta,H)} = \frac{2.3101}{0.7590} = 3.0436.$$

At subsequent times prior to hitting the barrier, the value of the paylater put is

$$BSPut\ (S_0,\ K,\ \sigma,\ r,T-t,\ \delta) - P \times DR(S_0,\ K,\ \sigma,\ r,T-t,\ \delta,\ H\ )$$

The paylater premium has the potential to be much lower than the COD premium. Compare a paylater with $H = K$ to a COD. You'll find in many cases that the COD premium is approximately twice as great. This is a consequence of the reflection principle—once you have hit the barrier, there is approximately a 50 percent chance that the option will move out of the money, which means that half the time, you'll pay the premium without the option paying off. Thus, the premium is half that of the COD, where the premium is always paid when and only when the option is in the money.

The initial delta will be $-0.1903 - 3.0436\ (-0.0439) = -0.0567$. The $DR$ has a gamma very close to zero; hence, initially, there is little difference between the paylater's gamma and a regular put option's gamma.

As time evolves the behavior of delta and gamma becomes similar to the COD, since in each case a small move can trigger a discrete payment; the main difference being that the discrete payment is likely to occur before expiration when $S_t$ gets close to the barrier.

### Question 23.4

We must show the formula is a solution to $e^{-r(T-t)}P\left(\overline{S}_T \geq H \text{ and } S_T < K\right)$ where $P$ stands for risk neutral probability.

We begin with the case when $H \geq K$ (i.e., the top equation). If the barrier is hit (i.e., $S = H$), $-d_4 = -d_2$, implying the probability is $N\ (-d_2) = P\ (S_T < K\ )$ (i.e., the risk neutral probability of receiving one dollar). If at time $T$, $\overline{S}_T \geq H$ and $S_T < K$, the barrier has been hit, and the probability is equal to $N\ (-d_2) = 1$. Lastly, if at time $T$, $\overline{S}_T < H$ or $S_T > K$, we must check to see if the probability is zero. If $S_T > K$ and the barrier has been hit, the probability becomes $N\ (-d_2) =$

0. If the barrier has not been hit (as a reminder $S_T > K$), then $S_T < H$ and $H^2/(S_T K) > 0$ implying $d_4 \to \infty$. The probability will be $\left(\frac{H}{S}\right)^k N(-d_4) = 0$.

For the case when $H < K$, if the barrier is hit $d_6 = d_8$ and $H$ drops out of the probability leaving $N(-d_2) = P(S_T < K)$. If at time $T$, $\overline{S}_T \geq H$ and $S_T < K$, the barrier has been hit and the probability is equal to $N(-d_2) = 1$. Finally, if at time $T$, $\overline{S}_T < H$ or $S_T > K$ we must check the probability is zero. If $S_T > K$ the barrier must have been hit and the probability is $N(-d_2) = 0$. If the barrier has not been hit (i.e., $\overline{S}_T < H$), then $S_T < H < K$. In this case $d_2 = d_6$ and $-d_8 = -\infty$, implying the probability equals zero.

## Question 23.6

Equivalently, we could use $x_0 Q_0 = 200$ as the stock price and set the dividend yield equal to $\delta_Q + \rho s \sigma_Q + r - r_f$. This gives $BSCall(200, 195, 0.15, 0.08, 1, 0.02 + 0.2 \times 0.1 \times 0.15 + 0.08 - 0.04) = \$15.319$.

## Question 23.8

The two dollar traded assets are $Y$ and $x$. Applying Proposition 20.4 to the ratio of these two yields

$$F_{t,T}\left(\frac{Y}{x}\right) = F_{t,T}(Y) F_{t,T}\left(\frac{1}{x}\right) e^{-\rho \sigma_Y s(T-t)}. \tag{6}$$

Note that $\rho$ is the correlation between $Y$ and $1/x$, which implies $\rho \sigma_Y s$ is the covariance given by equation (23.28). Since the forward price for $Y$ is $Y_t e^{(r - \delta_Q)(T-t)}$ and the forward price for $(1/x)$ is $(1/x_t) e^{\left(r_f - r + s^2\right)(T-t)}$ we have

$$F_{t,T}\left(\frac{Y}{x}\right) = Q_t e^{\left(r - \delta_Q + r_f - r + s^2 - \rho s \sigma_Q - s^2\right)(T-t)} = Q_t e^{\left(r_f - \delta_Q - \rho s \sigma_Q\right)(T-t)}. \tag{7}$$

The prepaid forward price is therefore $Q_t e^{\left(r_f - \delta_Q - \rho s \sigma_Q - r\right)(T-t)}$.

## Question 23.10

The value of the option is going to depend upon the probability that the stock at expiration will be greater than $K$, conditional on it having exceeded $H_1$ without ever having exceeded $H_2$.

One way to value an option like this is to use Monte Carlo simulation. By simulating the path of the stock price, we can isolate those paths along which we hit $H_1$ without hitting $H_2$.

However, we can also view this relatively complicated option as a *spread* of barrier options. Consider the following strategy:

- Buy an ordinary knock-in call with strike $K$ and barrier $H_1$

- Write an ordinary knock-in call with strike $K$ and barrier $H_2$

Now consider the payoffs given the different possible combinations of the stock hitting or not hitting the two barriers:

| Payoff | $H_1$ not hit | $H_1$ hit $H_2$ not hit | $H_1$ hit $H_2$ hit |
|---|---|---|---|
| Purchased knock-in | 0 | $Max(0, S_T - K)$ | $Max(0, S_T - K)$ |
| Written knock-in | 0 | 0 | $-Max(0, S_T - K)$ |
| Total | 0 | $Max(0, S_T - K)$ | 0 |

By entering into a knock-in spread, we are able to replicate the payoff to the knock-in, knock-out.[1]

## Question 23.12

a) If we plan to buy back the option at a predetermined stock price, we could implement this strategy mechanically by buying a knock-in call that knocks-in at the buy-back stock price. The buy-back price is the barrier. Thus, if we write a call intending to buy it back at a certain stock price, we have really written a knock-out call.

b) The knock-in call that we will buy at $45 to offset the written call has a premium

$$CallDownIn(50, 50, 0.3, 0.08, 1, 0, 45) = \$2.595$$

Thus, the net premium raised by selling the call in the first place is $7.856 - $2.595 = $5.261.

The use of a barrier option automatically offsets our written call position if the stock price hits the barrier. Thinking about the strategy this way has the benefit that we can determine *from the outset* the net premium we receive from writing the call: It is the call premium less the cost of the knock-in call.

---

[1]The easy pricing formula in this example relied on the fact that the knock-out price exceeded the knock-in price. There are also knock-in/knock-out options for which the stock price is *between* the knock-in and knock-out prices. For example if the current stock price is 100, we might have an option which knocks in at 80 and then knocks out at 120. These are not priced so easily, since we might hit the knock-out price before the option has knocked in. Numerical methods are required to price these options.

## Question 23.14

When using equation (23.47) for the lookback put, $\widetilde{S}_t = \overline{S}_t$ and $\omega = -1$.

a) If the stock is worthless, the put will be exercised at time $T$ and the holder will sell a worthless stock for $\overline{S}$ (which is known). This implies the lookback put should be worth the present value of $\overline{S}$. To verify, if $S_t = 0$, $\overline{S}$ will be greater than $S$, and the first term in equation (23.52) will be zero (since the term in brackets is bounded). The second term is $\overline{S}e^{-r(T-t)}N(-d_6')$. Since $S = 0$ and $\overline{S} > 0$, $d_6' \to -\infty$ implying $N(-d_6') \to 1$ and the lookback put is worth $\overline{S}e^{-r(T-t)}$.

b) At maturity if $S_T < \overline{S}_t$ then each $d_5' \to -\infty$ which implies $N(d_5') \to 0$ and both $N(-d_5')$ and $N(d_6') \to 1$. Similarly $d_8' \to \infty$, implying $N(-d_8') \to 0$. As a reminder $\omega = -1$; hence, equation (23.52) becomes

$$-S_T(1-0) + \overline{S}_t(1-0) = \overline{S}_t - S_T. \qquad (15)$$

If we happen to have $S_T = \underline{S}_T$, then each $d_i = 0$ and equation (23.52) becomes

$$-S_T\left(\frac{1}{2} - \frac{\sigma^2}{4(r-\delta)}\right) + \overline{S}_T\left(\left(\frac{1}{2} - \frac{\sigma^2}{4(r-\delta)}\right)\right) = 0 \qquad (16)$$

## Question 23.16

Let $y_t \equiv Q_0 \times S_t/Q_t$. If exercised, the option pays off

$$\left(S_t - S_0\frac{Q_t}{Q_0}\right)^+ m\left(\frac{S_t/S_0}{Q_t/Q_0}\right). \qquad (17)$$

where $m(\cdot)$ is the multiplier. We can rewrite the payoff as

$$\frac{Q_t}{Q_0}(y_t - S_0)^+ m(y_t) = \frac{Q_t}{Q_0}f(y_t). \qquad (18)$$

As in the exchange option, we can use Proposition 21.1 to value the $y$ payoff using a dividend yield of $r - \delta_Q$ and a volatility of $\sqrt{\sigma^2 + \sigma^2 - 2\rho\sigma\sigma_Q}$. This can be done with the binomial model with an "interest rate" of $\delta_Q$ since the risk neutral probability is

$$\frac{e^{(r-(r-\delta_Q))\Delta t} - d}{u - d} = \frac{e^{\delta_Q\Delta t} - d}{u - d}. \qquad (19)$$

Let $V(y_t)$ be this value, then Proposition 21.1 implies the Level 3 outperformance option will have a value of

$$\frac{Q_t^{e^{(r-\delta_Q)(T-t)}}}{Q_0} V(y_t). \tag{20}$$

This implies the current value (i.e., $t = 0$) of the option is simply $V(y_0)$. To find terminal value of the option, i.e., $V(y_T)$, we have to use the multiplier. For example, if the terminal node is $y(T) = 300$, then Level 3 will have outperformed the S&P by an annualized rate of $3^{0.25} - 1 = 0.3161$; since this is greater than 11 percent, we will receive a payoff of $(300 - 100) \times 8$. If the annualized rate is less than 11 percent (but greater than zero), we receive a payoff of $(y_T - 100) \times \frac{8}{11} \times 100$.

a)  See Table 1 for a 10-step binomial tree.

TABLE 1 (Problem 23.16a)

| Time (yrs) | 0.4 | 0.8 | 1.2 | 1.6 | 2 | 2.4 | 2.8 | 3.2 | 3.6 | 4 |
|---|---|---|---|---|---|---|---|---|---|---|
| 100 | 116.9995 | 136.8889 | 160.1594 | 187.3858 | 219.2405 | 256.5104 | 300.1161 | 351.1344 | 410.8257 | 480.6642 |
| | 240.7747 | 357.7046 | 515.7807 | 720.112 | 972.3534 | 1271.441 | 1618.023 | 2020.513 | 2492.345 | 3045.313 |
| | 86.7101 | 101.4504 | 118.6965 | 138.8744 | 162.4824 | 190.1037 | 222.4205 | 260.2309 | 304.469 | 356.2273 |
| | 88.3768 | 143.3498 | 226.4299 | 346.8114 | 512.6455 | 727.9501 | 990.1712 | 1293.285 | 1641.491 | 2049.819 |
| Value | | 75.18641 | 87.96775 | 102.9219 | 120.4181 | 140.8887 | 164.8391 | 192.861 | 225.6465 | 264.0054 |
| 157.74 | | 42.24001 | 73.75534 | 125.8406 | 208.7116 | 334.1874 | 511.9977 | 742.5413 | 1010.911 | 1312.043 |
| European Call | | | 65.19421 | 76.27692 | 89.24365 | 104.4147 | 122.1647 | 142.9321 | 167.2299 | 195.6583 |
| Strike = 100 | | | 15.67706 | 29.90796 | 56.19063 | 103.4985 | 185.6077 | 320.4118 | 521.4917 | 765.2662 |
| Vol = 23.69%; r = 1.80% | | | | 56.52996 | 66.13979 | 77.38326 | 90.53806 | 105.9291 | 123.9366 | 145.0052 |
| Exp = 4 years; Div = 0.00% | | | | 3.636767 | 7.6839 | 16.21976 | 34.20409 | 72.05331 | 151.6146 | 318.6434 |
| u = 1.170; d = 0.867 | | | | | 49.01718 | 57.34988 | 67.0991 | 78.50564 | 91.85124 | 107.4655 |
| Risk-neutral prob of up = 0.463 | | | | | 0.201573 | 0.438869 | 0.955515 | 2.080367 | 4.52942 | 9.861551 |
| | | | | | 42.50284 | 49.72813 | 58.18169 | 68.07231 | 79.6443 |
| | | | | | 0 | 0 | 0 | 0 | 0 |
| | | | | | | 36.85426 | 43.11931 | 50.4494 | 59.02557 |
| | | | | | | 0 | 0 | 0 | 0 |
| | | | | | | | 31.95636 | 37.3888 | 43.74472 |
| | | | | | | | 0 | 0 | 0 |
| | | | | | | | | 27.70939 | 32.41986 |
| | | | | | | | | 0 | 0 |
| | | | | | | | | | 24.02684 |
| | | | | | | | | | 0 |

b) See Table 2 for a 10-step binomial tree.

TABLE 2 (Problem 23.16b)

| Time (yrs) | 0.4 | 0.8 | 1.2 | 1.6 | 2 | 2.4 | 2.8 | 3.2 | 3.6 | 4 |
|---|---|---|---|---|---|---|---|---|---|---|
| 100 | 116.9995 | 136.8889 | 160.1594 | 187.3858 | 219.2405 | 256.5104 | 300.1161 | 351.1344 | 410.8257 | 480.6642 |
| | 240.8171 | 357.7704 | 515.8763 | 720.2369 | 972.4894 | 1271.539 | 1618.023 | 2020.513 | 2492.345 | 3045.313 |
| | 86.7101 | 101.4504 | 118.6965 | 138.8744 | 162.4824 | 190.1037 | 222.4205 | 260.2309 | 304.469 | 356.2273 |
| | 88.38895 | 143.3725 | 226.4711 | 346.8831 | 512.7625 | 728.12 | 990.3562 | 1293.285 | 1641.491 | 2049.819 |
| Value | | 75.18641 | 87.96775 | 102.9219 | 120.4181 | 140.8887 | 164.8391 | 192.861 | 225.6465 | 264.0054 |
| 157.77 | | 42.24326 | 73.76242 | 125.856 | 208.7452 | 334.2605 | 512.156 | 742.8879 | 1010.911 | 1312.043 |

| | 0.4 | 0.8 | 1.2 | 1.6 | 2 | 2.4 | 2.8 | 3.2 | 3.6 | 4 |
|---|---|---|---|---|---|---|---|---|---|---|
| American Call | | | 65.19421 | 76.27692 | 89.24365 | 104.4147 | 122.1647 | 142.9321 | 167.2299 | 195.6583 |
| Strike = 100 | | | 15.67706 | 29.90796 | 56.19063 | 103.4985 | 185.6077 | 320.4118 | 521.4917 | 765.2662 |
| Vol = 23.69%; r = 1.80% | | | | 56.52996 | 66.13979 | 77.38326 | 90.53806 | 105.9291 | 123.9366 | 145.0052 |
| Exp = 4 years; Div = 0.00% | | | | 3.636767 | 7.6839 | 16.21976 | 34.20409 | 72.05331 | 151.6146 | 318.6434 |
| u = 1.170; d = 0.867 | | | | | 49.01718 | 57.34988 | 67.0991 | 78.50564 | 91.85124 | 107.4655 |
| Risk-neutral prob of up = 0.463 | | | | | 0.201573 | 0.438869 | 0.955515 | 2.080367 | 4.52942 | 9.861551 |
| | | | | | | 42.50284 | 49.72813 | 58.18169 | 68.07231 | 79.6443 |
| | | | | | | 0 | 0 | 0 | 0 | 0 |
| | | | | | | | 36.85426 | 43.11931 | 50.4494 | 59.02557 |
| | | | | | | | 0 | 0 | 0 | 0 |
| | | | | | | | | 31.95636 | 37.3888 | 43.74472 |
| | | | | | | | | 0 | 0 | 0 |
| | | | | | | | | | 27.70939 | 32.41986 |
| | | | | | | | | | 0 | 0 |
| | | | | | | | | | | 24.02684 |
| | | | | | | | | | | 0 |

c) Notice early exercise in the middle of the American tree. If the option is deep in the money, standard arguments make early exercise suboptimal. We have a multiplier of 8 since there is a "cushion" (i.e., little risk of falling below the 11 percent cap). However, when we are just over the 11 percent cap, if the stock price falls, we will lose out since the multiplier will fall. Since Level 3 pays no dividends, the multiplier is central to early exercise. If there was no multiplier, there would be no incentive to have early exercise since we essentially exchanging a dividend paying asset for a non-dividend paying asset.

# Chapter 24

## Volatility

**Question 24.2**

|  | SP500 | IBM | Xerox |
|---|---|---|---|
| 12/31/1991 | 14.07% | 24.02% | 27.57% |
| 12/31/1992 | 9.57% | 27.80% | 20.60% |
| 12/31/1993 | 8.55% | 29.54% | 21.60% |
| 12/30/1994 | 9.76% | 29.58% | 22.31% |
| 12/29/1995 | 8.01% | 23.21% | 22.47% |
| 12/31/1996 | 11.60% | 33.58% | 32.79% |
| 12/31/1997 | 18.17% | 35.03% | 28.21% |
| 12/31/1998 | 20.03% | 30.23% | 36.02% |
| 12/31/1999 | 17.76% | 41.94% | 57.90% |
| 12/29/2000 | 21.63% | 48.21% | 84.43% |
| 12/31/2001 | 20.39% | 35.38% | 78.51% |
| 12/31/2002 | 25.95% | 42.41% | 67.92% |
| 12/31/2003 | 16.46% | 22.38% | 39.65% |
| 12/31/2004 | 10.93% | 14.42% | 26.23% |
| Overall | 16.45% | 32.91% | 46.63% |

The results of the daily volatility calculations are remarkably similar to the weekly volatility calculations. We have the same time-series variation, and the magnitudes of most of the calculated volatilities are similar.

## Question 24.4

Here is the code you can use for a common statistical package, STATA:

```
Stata commands:

insheet using C:\garch_ibm.txt
tsset seqn
arch ret, arch(1/1) garch(1/1)
predict var, variance
```

This code produces the following results:

```
---------------------------------------------------------------------------
         ret |    Coef.    Std. Err.      z     P>|z|     [ 95% Conf. Interval]
-------------+-------------------------------------------------------------
ARCH         |
        arch |
         B2. |   .0440766   .0047828     9.22   0.000     .0347026    .0534507
       garch |
         B3. |   .9556661   .0053281   179.36   0.000     .9452231    .966109
          B1 |   1.34e-06   1.03e-06     1.30   0.193    -6.77e-07   3.36e-06
---------------------------------------------------------------------------
```

You can see that the results are very close to the estimates reported in the book.

The following graph plots the annualized volatility based on the Garch (1, 1) estimates—you should do this as well for your estimates of B1, B2, and B3, and compare it with the graph of the main textbook. They should look very similar.

### Garch (1, 1) volatility for BM, Jan 1999 - Dec 2003

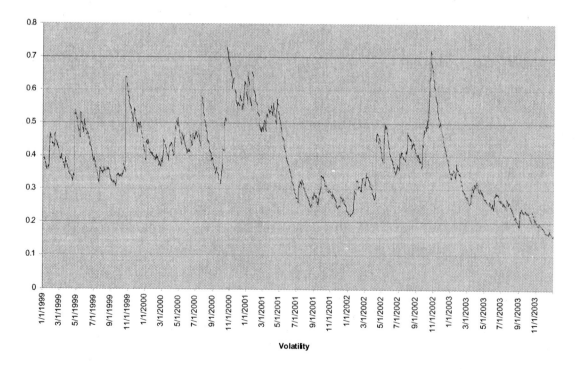

Volatility

If we exclude the four daily absolute returns above 12 percent, we obtain the following estimates:

```
------------------------------------------------------------------------
       ret |     Coef.   Std. Err.      z     P>|z|   [ 95% Conf. Interval]
-----------+------------------------------------------------------------
-----------+------------------------------------------------------------
ARCH       |
      arch |
       B2. |   .0472975   .0066992     7.06   0.000    .0341673   .0604277
     garch |
       B3. |   .9499507   .0075384   126.01   0.000    .9351757   .9647258
        B1 |   1.89e-06   1.26e-06     1.50   0.133   -5.73e-07   4.35e-06
------------------------------------------------------------------------
```

While the coefficients are a bit different from the ones in the book, we can calculate an unconditional volatility of:

$$\sqrt{\frac{0.00000189}{1-0.047295-0.9499507} \times 252} = 0.416,$$

which is very similar to the estimate of 0.4229 in the textbook.

## Question 24.6

Here is a table of volatilities and the corresponding option prices for the problem.

| Volatility | Option Price |
|---|---|
| 0.05 | 50.02999100179970 |
| 0.1 | 50.02999100179970 |
| 0.15 | 50.02999100179970 |
| 0.2 | 50.02999100179970 |
| 0.25 | 50.02999100179970 |
| 0.3 | 50.02999100179970 |
| 0.35 | 50.02999100179970 |
| 0.4 | 50.02999100179970 |
| 0.45 | 50.02999100179970 |
| 0.5 | 50.02999100179970 |
| 0.55 | 50.02999100179970 |
| 0.6 | 50.02999100179970 |
| 0.65 | 50.02999100179970 |
| 0.7 | 50.02999100179970 |
| 0.75 | 50.02999100179970 |
| 0.8 | 50.02999100179970 |

| Volatility | Option Price |
|---|---|
| 0.85 | 50.02999100179970 |
| 0.9 | 50.02999100179970 |
| 0.95 | 50.02999100179980 |
| 1 | 50.02999100180160 |
| 5 | 51.33309337854208 |

We can see that at a volatility of 30 percent, the option price is indeed 50.02999. The vega at a volatility of 30 percent is $2.129510350240270e - 116$, or virtually zero. Vega is measuring the sensitivity of the option price with respect to a change in the volatility. Note that we only have very little time left to maturity. Even if there is a lot of volatility, it will not be able to move the stock price significantly over such a short period of time. Only if we choose a very high volatility of 500 percent, we see that the stock price moves a significant amount.

This demonstrates that it is very difficult, if not impossible, to calculate implied volatilities for deep in-the-money call options with short maturities.

## Question 24.8

This is a snapshot from the spreadsheet:

| Inputs | | Black-Scholes (European) | Call | Put |
|---|---|---|---|---|
| Stock Price | 50 | Price | 3E-119 | 49.94002 |
| Exercise Price | 100 | Delta | 4.6E-118 | -1 |
| Volatility | 30.000% | Gamma | 7.2E-117 | 7.2E-117 |
| Risk-free interest rate | 6.000% | Vega | 5.4E-118 | 5.4E-118 |
| Time to Expiration (years) | 0.01 | Theta | -2E-117 | 0.016428 |
| Dividend Yield | 0.000% | Rho | 2.3E-120 | -0.00999 |
| # Binomial steps | 4 | Elasticity | 772.8687 | -1.0012 |
| Type (0=Eur, 1=Amer) | 0 | | | |

a) We can see from above that the price of the option is zero.

b) We can see from the spreadsheet that the vega is indeed zero. A small, local change in volatility does not have any impact on the option price, because the stock price needs to change by more than $50 in 0.01 years for the option to pay off a positive amount of money.

c) For the bid, we obtain an implied volatility of 29.94 percent, for the ask, we obtain an implied volatility of 285.25 percent. The logic behind the implied volatility for the ask is that the stock price needs to be able to move a considerable amount in a short time to make the option worth more than zero.

d) Market makers are obligated to make a market in the option, so they have to quote prices even in such an option. The market maker obviously does not want to pay for such an option that is virtually guaranteed to pay off nothing, so that explains the bid price of zero. The ask price might be explained by the market maker wanting to make a small profit, and by some fear that the stock price might rally.

e) The same conclusions as for deep-in-the-money options with extremely short maturity hold—interpretations should be made very cautiously. In academic studies relating to implied volatilities, you often see bounds on moneyness ($S/K$) and time to maturity when researchers are estimating an implied volatility curve.

## Question 24.10

You can see from the figure below that we observe an implied volatility smile for IBM options. We also learn that the implied volatility curve for the call bid prices is not well behaved.

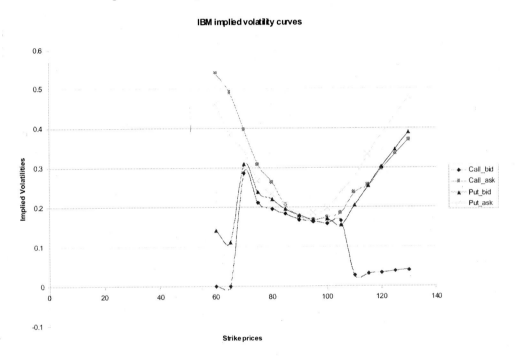

# Question 24.12

Here is a table with all implied volatilities for parts (a), (b) and (c):

| Call /Put | Strike | part a) | | part b) | | part c) | |
|---|---|---|---|---|---|---|---|
| | | bid_implied | ask_implied | bid_implied | ask_implied | bid_implied | ask_implied |
| C | 30 | #VALUE! | #VALUE! | 58.6% | 61.3% | 57.2% | 60.1% |
| P | 30 | 14.4% | 49.0% | 14.1% | 44.7% | 12.6% | 44.7% |
| C | 40 | #VALUE! | #VALUE! | 41.0% | 45.0% | 39.5% | 43.9% |
| P | 40 | 34.0% | 39.4% | 33.8% | 36.9% | 33.8% | 36.9% |
| C | 50 | #VALUE! | #VALUE! | 32.5% | 34.4% | 31.5% | 33.6% |
| P | 50 | 31.1% | 33.3% | 30.8% | 32.0% | 30.8% | 32.0% |
| C | 60 | #VALUE! | 21.8% | 28.5% | 29.4% | 28.0% | 29.0% |
| P | 60 | 28.4% | 29.4% | 28.0% | 28.6% | 28.1% | 28.6% |
| C | 70 | 21.6% | 23.6% | 25.5% | 26.3% | 25.2% | 26.1% |
| P | 70 | 26.1% | 26.7% | 25.7% | 26.0% | 25.7% | 26.0% |
| C | 80 | 21.3% | 22.8% | 23.2% | 23.9% | 23.1% | 23.8% |
| P | 80 | 23.9% | 24.6% | 23.3% | 23.7% | 23.4% | 23.7% |
| C | 85 | 21.0% | 21.9% | 22.4% | 22.9% | 22.3% | 22.8% |
| P | 85 | 23.1% | 23.7% | 22.4% | 22.7% | 22.5% | 22.8% |
| C | 90 | 20.7% | 21.3% | 21.8% | 22.1% | 21.8% | 22.0% |
| P | 90 | 22.5% | 23.1% | 21.7% | 22.0% | 21.8% | 22.1% |
| C | 95 | 20.1% | 20.7% | 21.1% | 21.3% | 21.0% | 21.3% |
| P | 95 | 22.1% | 22.6% | 21.1% | 21.4% | 21.2% | 21.5% |
| C | 100 | 19.6% | 20.1% | 20.3% | 20.6% | 20.3% | 20.6% |
| P | 100 | 21.8% | 22.3% | 20.6% | 20.9% | 20.7% | 21.0% |
| C | 110 | 19.0% | 19.6% | 19.6% | 19.9% | 19.6% | 19.8% |
| P | 110 | 21.9% | 22.9% | 20.1% | 20.6% | 20.2% | 20.7% |
| C | 120 | 18.1% | 19.3% | 18.5% | 19.1% | 18.5% | 19.1% |
| P | 120 | 23.9% | 24.7% | 21.2% | 21.7% | 21.4% | 21.9% |
| C | 130 | 18.0% | 19.1% | 18.3% | 18.9% | 18.3% | 18.9% |
| P | 130 | 27.2% | 28.6% | 23.8% | 24.7% | 24.1% | 25.0% |
| C | 140 | 16.8% | 19.5% | 17.1% | 18.7% | 17.1% | 18.6% |
| P | 140 | 31.3% | 32.7% | 27.7% | 28.6% | 27.9% | 28.9% |
| C | 150 | 19.2% | 22.1% | 19.5% | 21.2% | 19.4% | 21.2% |

| Call /Put | Strike | part a) | | part b) | | part c) | |
|---|---|---|---|---|---|---|---|
| P | 150 | 35.5% | 37.0% | 31.8% | 32.8% | 32.1% | 33.1% |

a) Note that we cannot calculate implied volatilities for some of the deep-in-the-money call options.

b) We have to find all dividends for 2004 and discount them appropriately. Note that we make the assumption here that we had perfect foresight about the dividends: We use dividends for all of 2004, although we are calculating option prices on January 12, 2004. This is not possible in real life, and you would have to make the assumption that past dividends are a good proxy for future dividends.

We have:

| | amount | date | days to maturity | discounted at 2% |
|---|---|---|---|---|
| Div1 | 0.16 | 3/10/2004 | 58 | 0.159492 |
| Div2 | 0.18 | 6/10/2004 | 150 | 0.178527 |
| Div3 | 0.18 | 9/10/2004 | 242 | 0.177629 |
| Div4 | 0.18 | 12/10/2004 | 333 | 0.176745 |
| Total | | | | 0.692393 |

We correct the IBM stock price of $91.55 by $0.6924 to $90.8576 and use that price in the volatility calculations. Most notably, you should see that you can now calculate implied volatilities for the low-strike options from part (a).

c) We have to calculate an annualized dividend rate. In 2003, we had the following dividend payments:

| date | amount |
|---|---|
| 3/10/2003 | 0.15 |
| 6/10/2003 | 0.16 |
| 9/10/2003 | 0.16 |
| 12/10/2003 | 0.16 |
| Total | 0.63 |

We obtain a dividend yield of 0.69 percent (0.63 / 91.55). The implied volatilities are quite close for parts (b) and (c), so it does not make a big difference which dividend adjustment model we use.

d) Look at the following figure:

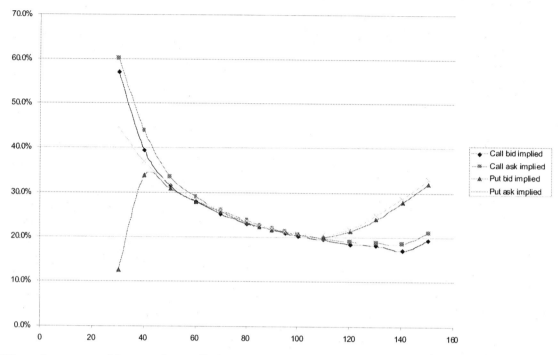

One-year IBM Options - Implied Volatilites

There is some evidence of a smile in put options, although for call options, it looks more like a smirk.

## Question 24.14

| | $5-step | strike in [60,200] | $1-step | $10-step |
|---|---|---|---|---|
| forward price | 108.329 | 108.329 | 108.329 | 108.329 |
| K0 | 105 | 105 | 108 | 100 |
| sum(put-term) | 0.0467 | 0.0459 | 0.0489 | 0.0413 |
| sum(call-term) | 0.0431 | 0.0428 | 0.0410 | 0.0488 |
| F(0,T) adjustment | 0.00101 | 0.00101 | 0.00001 | 0.00694 |
| Sigma2Vix | 0.089 | 0.088 | 0.090 | 0.083 |
| Sigma Vix | 0.298 | 0.296 | 0.300 | 0.288 |

We know that the true implied volatility is equal to 30 percent—after all, we created the prices! We learn from the table that the wider the dispersion of strike prices, the more accurate the calculation of VIX (Compare columns 1 and 2). We also learn that the finer the grid of strike prices, the more accurate the calculation of VIX. In fact, we know that the formula is true for continuous strike prices, but the $1 approximation works already very accurately up to the fourth decimal. You can see that the $10 distance in strikes (column 4) does not work as well—we are 1.2 percentage points away from the true implied volatility.

## Question 24.16

This is a difficult exercise. The most difficult part is to set up the spreadsheet for the infinite sum in the formula 21.60. Note that we divide by factorial($i$), so that the weight decays very quickly. You should be alright to sum up to a value of $i = 50$, and ignore all other terms. Also note from Chapter 19 that

$$k = e^{\alpha_j} - 1$$

In order to set up the spreadsheet, enter in column A the indicator $i$ ($i = 1$ to 50), define in column B the exponential weights, and in columns C to W, enter the strike prices from 50 to 150. Then, for each strike, sum over all 50 rows.

Stop reading here now if you did not find the solution and try again; it is worth it.

Here are the values for the first four strike prices for the implied volatility (using the BSCallImpVol function that comes with the spreadsheet), backed out from the generated Merton Jump Diffusion prices:

| K | 50 | 55 | 60 | 65 |
|---|---|---|---|---|
| a_j = −0.2, s_j = 0.3 | 0.3457 | 0.3334 | 0.3248 | 0.3190 |
| a_j = −0.4, s_j = 0.3 | 0.3623 | 0.3464 | 0.3348 | 0.3266 |
| a_j = −0.1, s_j = 0.3 | 0.3382 | 0.3276 | 0.3205 | 0.3159 |
| a_j = −0.2, s_j = 0.1 | 0.3183 | 0.3137 | 0.3107 | 0.3086 |
| a_j = −0.2, s_j = 0.4 | 0.3645 | 0.3475 | 0.3352 | 0.3268 |
| lambda = 0.01 | 0.3273 | 0.3187 | 0.3133 | 0.3099 |
| lambda = 0.05 | 0.3831 | 0.3663 | 0.3530 | 0.3428 |

The implied volatility curve for the different prices looks like this:

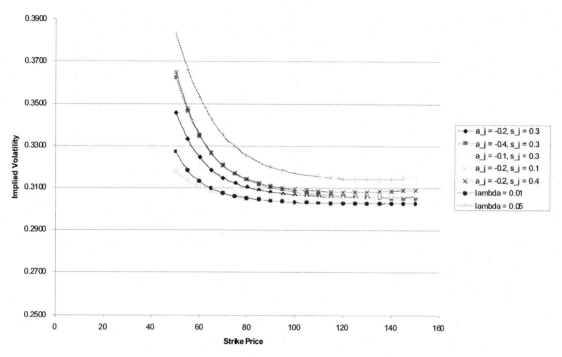

Implied Volatilities from the Merton Jump - Diffusion Model for different parameter values

The steepest curve is created for lambda = 0.05, the flattest "smirk" is created when sigma_j = 0.1.

## Question 24.18

Here is a graph of the implied volatility estimations:

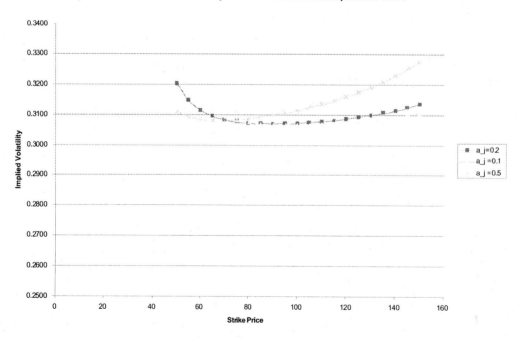

Implied Volatilities from the Merton Jump- Diffusion Model for different parameter values

The main point is that the implied volatility smirk can "smirk" in the other direction if we make the jump magnitude positive enough (see the upwards sloping curve for alpha($j$) = 0.5.

## Question 24.20

We get the following prices from the CEV model:

| | $t = 0.25$ | $t = 0.5$ | $t = 1$ | $t = 2$ |
|---|---|---|---|---|
| 60 | 41.1881 | 42.3589 | 44.6969 | 49.2451 |
| 65 | 36.2882 | 37.581 | 40.2262 | 45.3347 |
| 70 | 31.3963 | 32.8632 | 35.8988 | 41.6058 |
| 75 | 26.5425 | 28.2761 | 31.7775 | 38.0881 |
| 80 | 21.8053 | 23.9145 | 27.9192 | 34.8017 |
| 85 | 17.3231 | 19.8784 | 24.3671 | 31.7566 |
| 90 | 13.2674 | 16.2511 | 21.147 | 28.9545 |
| 95 | 9.7874 | 13.084 | 18.2674 | 26.3904 |
| 100 | 6.9632 | 10.392 | 15.7222 | 24.0543 |
| 105 | 4.791 | 8.1581 | 13.4945 | 21.9332 |
| 110 | 3.1997 | 6.3422 | 11.5602 | 20.012 |
| 115 | 2.0827 | 4.8916 | 9.8913 | 18.275 |
| 120 | 1.3266 | 3.7495 | 8.4585 | 16.7062 |
| 125 | 0.8302 | 2.8606 | 7.2331 | 15.2902 |
| 130 | 0.5122 | 2.1752 | 6.1879 | 14.0125 |
| 135 | 0.3125 | 1.6505 | 5.298 | 12.8593 |
| 140 | 0.1891 | 1.2509 | 4.5412 | 11.818 |

The resulting implied volatility curve is now upward sloping.

# Chapter 25

## Interest Rate and Bond Derivatives

### Question 25.2

a)  The two-year forward price is $F = P(0, 3) / P(0, 2) = 0.7722/0.8495 = 0.90901$.

b)  Since $FP(0, 2) = P(0, 3)$ the first input into the formula will be 0.7722. The present value of the strike price is $0.9P(0, 2) = 0.9 \times 0.8495 = 0.76455$. We can use this as the strike with no interest rate; we could also use a strike of 0.9 with an interest rate equal to the two-year yield. Either way the option is worth

$$BSCall\,(0.7722, 0.76455, 0.105, 0, 2, 0) = \$0.0494 \tag{3}$$

c)  Using put call parity for futures options,

$$p = c + KP(0, 2) - FP(0, 2) = 0.0494 + 0.76455 - 0.7722 = \$0.4175. \tag{4}$$

d)  The caplet is worth 1.11 two-year put options with strike $1/1.11 = 0.9009$. The no-interest formula will use $(0.9009)(0.8495) = 0.7653$ as the strike. The caplet has a value of

$$1.11 BSPut\,(0.7722, 0.7653, 0.105, 0, 2, 0) = \$0.0468. \tag{5}$$

### Question 25.4

A flat yield curve implies the two bond prices are $P_1 = e^{-0.08(3)} = 0.78663$ and $P_2 = e^{-0.08(6)} = 0.61878$. If we have purchased the three-year bond, the duration hedge is a position of

$$N = -\frac{1}{2}\frac{P_1}{P_2} = -\frac{1}{2}e^{3(0.08)} = -0.63562 \tag{7}$$

in the six-year bond. Notice the total cost of this strategy is

$$V_{8\%} = 0.78663 - 0.63562\,(0.61878) = 0.39332, \tag{8}$$

which implies we will owe $0.39332e^{0.08/365} = 0.39341$ in one day. If yields rise to 8.25 percent, our portfolio will have a value

$$V_{8.25\%} = e^{-0.0825(3-1/365)} - 0.63562e^{-0.0825(6-1/365)} = 0.39338. \tag{9}$$

If yields fall to 7.75 percent, the value will be

$$V_{7.75\%} = e^{-0.0775(3-1/365)} - 0.63562e^{-0.0775(6-1/365)} = 0.39338. \tag{10}$$

Either way we lose 0.00003. This is a binomial version of the impossibility of a no arbitrage flat (stochastic) yield curve.

## Question 25.6

Note that the interest rate risk premium of zero implies $\varphi = 0$.

a)  Beginning with the CIR model and using equation (25.34),

$$\gamma = \sqrt{a^2 + 2\sigma^2} = \sqrt{0.2^2 + 2(0.44721)^2} = 0.66332. \tag{18}$$

Let $A_2$ and $B_2$ be the two-year bond's $A$ and $B$ term in equation (25.34). Then

$$A_2 = \left( \frac{2\gamma e^{2+\gamma}}{(0.2+\gamma)(e^{2\gamma}-1)+2\gamma} \right)^{0.04/0.44721^2} = 0.96718 \tag{19}$$

and

$$B_2 = \frac{2(e^{2\gamma}-1)}{(0.2+\gamma)(e^{2\gamma}-1)+2\gamma} = 1.4897. \tag{20}$$

This gives a price of the two-year bond equal to

$$P(0, 2) = 0.96718e^{-1.4897(0.05)} = 0.89776. \tag{21}$$

The delta is $P_r = -B_2 P(0, 2) = -1.4897(0.89776) = -1.3374$, and the gamma is $P_{rr} = B_2^2 P(0, 2) = 1.4897(0.89776) = 1.9923$. Similar analysis for the ten-year bond will yield a price of $P(0, 10) = 0.6107$, a delta of $-1.4119$, and a gamma of 3.2643. The "true" duration of the bonds should be $-P_r/P$, which equal 1.49 and 2.31 (respectively) quite different from 2 and 10 years. The "true" convexity should be $P_{rr}/P$, which equals 2.22 and 5.35; the traditional convexities are $P_{yy}/P = 4$ and 100.

Using similar notation for the Vasicek model and equation (25.31), the two-year bond price is derived from the components

$$r = 0.1 - 0.5\ 0.1^2 / 0.2^2 = -0.025, \tag{22}$$

$$B_2 = 1 - e^{-2(0.2)} / 0.2 = 1.6484, \tag{23}$$

and

$$A_2 = e^{-0.025(1.6484-2)-0.16484/0.8} = 0.97514. \tag{24}$$

The two-year bond will be worth $P(0, 2) = 0.97514e^{-1.6484(0.05)} = 0.89799$. As in the CIR analysis, the delta will be $P_r = -B_2 P(0, 2) = -1.6484\ (0.89799) = -1.4802$ and a gamma of $P_{rr} = B_2^2 P(0, 2) = 1.6484^2(0.89799) = 2.44$. Similarly, the price of the 10-year bond is 0.735, the delta is $-3.1776$, and the gamma is 13.74. The "true" durations $-P_r/P$ are 1.65 and 4.32, which are substantially different from 2 and 10. The convexity measures $P_{rr}/P$, which equal 2.72 and 18.694, are also quite different from 4 and 100.

b) The duration hedge will use a position of

$$N_{duration} = -\frac{2}{10}\frac{P(0,2)}{P(0,10)} = -0.2(0.89799)/0.735 = -0.24435. \tag{25}$$

The delta hedge is

$$N_{delta} = -\frac{P_r(0,2)}{P(0,10)} = -\frac{1.4802}{3.177} = -0.4658. \tag{26}$$

The duration hedged portfolio has a cost of $0.89799 - 0.24435\,(0.735) = 0.71839$ and the delta hedge costs $0.89799 - 0.4658\,(0.735) = 0.55563$. The one-day standard deviation for $r$ will be $0.05 \pm 0.1/\sqrt{365}$. In the "up" scenario, the bond prices will become $P_2 = 0.8904$ and $P_{10} = 0.7186$. The return in the up scenario for the two hedges are

$$return_{duration} = 0.8904 - 0.24435\,(0.7186) - 0.71839e^{0.05/365} = -0.00368 \tag{27}$$

and

$$return_{delta} = 0.8904 - 0.4658\,(0.7186) - 0.55563e^{0.05/365} = -0.00003. \tag{28}$$

In the "down" scenario, the bond prices will be $P_2 = 0.905895$ and $P_{10} = 0.751818$. The return in the down scenario for the two hedges are

$$return_{duration} = 0.905895 - 0.24435\,(0.751818) - 0.71839e^{0.05/365} = 0.0037 \tag{29}$$

and

$$return_{delta} = 0.905895 - 0.4658\,(0.751818) - 0.55563e^{0.05/365} = -0.00009. \tag{30}$$

The delta hedge error is significantly smaller (in absolute terms) in both scenarios.

c) The one-day standard deviation for the CIR model is $\sigma_{CIR}\sqrt{r/365} = 5.2342 \times 10^{-3}$ which is, by design, the same as part (b). The duration hedge is

$$N_{duration} = -\frac{2}{10}\frac{P(0,2)}{P(0,10)} = -0.2\frac{0.89776}{0.6107} = -0.29401. \tag{31}$$

which has a total cost of $0.89776 - 0.29401\,(0.6107) = 0.71821$. The delta hedge is

$$N_{delta} = -\frac{P_r(0,2)}{P_r(0,10)} = -\frac{1.3374}{1.4119} = -0.94723, \tag{32}$$

which has a total cost of $0.89776 - 0.94723\,(0.6107) = 0.3193$. If $r$ rises by the one-day standard deviation, the bond prices will be $P_2 = 0.89092$ and $P_{10} = 0.603436$. This leads to "up" returns of

$$return_{duration} = 0.89092 - 0.29401\,(0.6034) - 0.71821e^{0.05/365} = -0.0048 \tag{33}$$

and

$$return_{delta} = 0.89092 - 0.94723\,(0.6034) - 0.3193e^{0.05/365} = -6.42 \times 10^{-6}. \qquad (34)$$

If the short-term rate falls by the one-day standard deviation, the bond prices will be $P_2 = 0.9049$ and $P_{10} = 0.6182$, leading to "down" returns of

$$return_{duration} = 0.9049 - 0.2940\,(0.6182) - 0.71821e^{0.05/365} = 0.0048. \qquad (35)$$

and

$$return_{delta} = 0.9049 - 0.94723\,(0.6182) - 0.3193e^{0.05/365} = -2.13 \times 10^{-5}. \qquad (36)$$

Without rounding errors the return is closer to $-6 \times 10^{-6}$.

## Question 25.8

Instead of one, long equation, we will work backwards. In Year 3, the four-year bond is worth the same value as the one-year bond in the terminal nodes of Figure 25.6. In Year 2, the bond will be worth three possible values, $0.8321\left(\frac{0.8331+0.8644}{2}\right) = 0.70624$, $0.8798\left(\frac{0.8644+0.8906}{2}\right) = 0.77202$, or $0.9153\frac{(0.8906+0.9123)}{2} = 0.8251$. In Year 1, the bond will be worth two possible values, $0.8832\left(\frac{0.70624+0.77202}{2}\right) = 0.6528$ or $0.9023\left(\frac{0.77202+0.8251}{2}\right) = 0.72054$ discounted expected value. Finally, the current value is the

$$P(0,4) = 0.9091\left(\frac{0.6528+0.72054}{2}\right) = 0.6243. \qquad (42)$$

## Question 25.10

The value of the Year 2 cap payment has been shown to be $V_2 = 1.958$. We must add to this the value of the Year 3 cap payment and the value of the Year 1 cap payment. In Year 2, the Year 3 cap payment will be worth three possible values: $0.8321\left(\frac{6.689+3.184}{2}\right) = 4.1077$, $0.8798\left(\frac{3.184+0.25}{2}\right) = 1.5106$, or $0.9153\,(0.125) = 0.11441$. In Year 1, the Year 3 cap payment will be worth two possible values: $0.8832\left(\frac{4.1077+1.5106}{2}\right) = 2.481$ or $0.9023\left(\frac{1.5106+0.11441}{2}\right) = 0.73312$. Hence the Year 3 cap payment has a current value of

$$V_3 = 0.9091\left(\frac{2.481+0.73312}{2}\right) = 1.461. \qquad (44)$$

The Year 1 cap payment has a value of $V_1 = 0.9091\left(\frac{1.078}{2}\right) = 0.49$. Summing the three, we have

$$V_1 + V_2 + V_3 = 0.49 + 1.958 + 1.461 = 3.909. \qquad (45)$$

## Question 25.12

See Table 2 for the bond prices, which are the same for the two trees. The one-year bonds are simply $1/(1+r)$, where $r$ is the short rate from the given trees. For the two-year bonds, we can solve recursively with formulas such as $B(0,2) = B(0,1) \times \left[ \frac{B(0,1)_u + B(0,1)_d}{2} \right]$ where $B(0,1)$ is the node's one-year bond and $B(0,1)_u$ and $B(0,1)_d$ are the one-year bond prices at the next node. Once we have two-year bonds, three-year bond values can be given by $B(0,3) = B(0,1) \times \left[ \frac{B(0,2)_u + B(0,2)_d}{2} \right]$ and similarly for the four- and five-year bonds.

## Table 2 (Problem 25.12)

Tree #1

| 0.08 | 0.07676 | 0.0817 | 0.07943 | 0.07552 |
|------|---------|--------|---------|---------|
|      | 0.10362 | 0.10635 | 0.09953 | 0.09084 |
|      |         | 0.13843 | 0.12473 | 0.10927 |
|      |         |        | 0.1563 | 0.13143 |
|      |         |        |        | 0.15809 |

Tree #2

| 0.08 | 0.08112 | 0.08749 | 0.08261 | 0.07284 |
|------|---------|---------|---------|---------|
|      | 0.09908 | 0.10689 | 0.10096 | 0.08907 |
|      |         | 0.1306 | 0.12338 | 0.10891 |
|      |         |        | 0.15078 | 0.13317 |
|      |         |        |        | 0.16283 |

One Year Bond Prices

Tree #1

| **0.925926** | 0.928712 | 0.924471 | 0.926415 | 0.929783 |
|------|---------|--------|---------|---------|
|      | 0.906109 | 0.903873 | 0.90948 | 0.916725 |
|      |         | 0.878403 | 0.889102 | 0.901494 |
|      |         |        | 0.864827 | 0.883837 |
|      |         |        |        | 0.863491 |

Tree #2

| **0.925926** | 0.924967 | 0.919549 | 0.923694 | 0.932105 |
|------|---------|--------|---------|---------|
|      | 0.909852 | 0.903432 | 0.908298 | 0.918215 |
|      |         | 0.884486 | 0.890171 | 0.901786 |
|      |         |        | 0.868976 | 0.88248 |
|      |         |        |        | 0.859971 |

Two Year Bond Prices

Tree #1

| **0.849454** | 0.849002 | 0.848615 | 0.855316 |
|------|---------|--------|---------|
|      | 0.807468 | 0.812845 | 0.826816 |
|      |         | 0.770328 | 0.793671 |
|      |         |        | 0.755569 |

Tree #2

| **0.849453** | 0.843098 | 0.842303 | 0.854564 |
|------|---------|--------|---------|
|      | 0.81337 | 0.812397 | 0.826552 |
|      |         | 0.77797 | 0.794151 |
|      |         |        | 0.757074 |

Three Year Bond Prices

Tree #1

| **0.766885** | 0.771509 | 0.777541 |
|------|---------|--------|
|      | 0.717264 | 0.732357 |
|      |         | 0.680428 |

Tree #2

| **0.766884** | 0.765271 | 0.772934 |
|------|---------|--------|
|      | 0.7235 | 0.732097 |
|      |         | 0.686018 |

Four Year Bond Prices

Tree #1

| **0.689247** | 0.70113 |
|------|--------|
|      | 0.640069 |

Tree #2

| **0.689246** | 0.696052 |
|------|--------|
|      | 0.645138 |

Five Year Bond Price

Tree #1

**0.620926**

Tree #2

**0.620921**

## Question 25.14

See Table 4 for the numerical answers to parts (a) and (b). Let $r_f(i)$ and $r_e(i)$ be the one-period forward rate for borrowing at time $i$.

### Table 4 (Problem 25.14)

| 1 year forward rate | American | European | Difference |
|---|---|---|---|
| Year 2 | 9.002% | 9.019% | 0.017% |
| Year 3 | 10.767% | 10.803% | 0.036% |
| Year 4 | 11.264% | 11.308% | 0.044% |
| Year 5 | 11.003% | 11.041% | 0.037% |

| 1 year forward rate | American | European | Difference |
|---|---|---|---|
| Year 2 | 9.003% | 9.003% | 0.000% |
| Year 3 | 10.767% | 10.788% | 0.021% |
| Year 4 | 11.264% | 11.299% | 0.035% |
| Year 5 | 11.004% | 11.048% | 0.044% |

Year 3 European Calculations
0.0917689  0.087322
0.110899
**0.10803279**

Year 3 European Calculations
0.0916379  0.089898
0.10804
**0.10787872**

Year 4 European Calculations
0.08671898  0.085475  0.082722
0.101838  0.101351
**0.11307958**  0.123429

Year 4 European Calculations
0.08664816  0.085901  0.084401
0.101259  0.101338
**0.11298736**  0.121245

Year 5 European Calculations
0.07609656  0.077625  0.077682  0.077059
0.086744  0.089484  0.090998
**0.11040541**  0.101981  0.107003
0.125192

Year 5 European Calculations
0.07614931  0.076312  0.07572  0.074778
0.08817  0.089286  0.089912
**0.11048209**  0.104526  0.107746
0.128608

a) Note the forward rates only depend on the initial bond prices; for example, $r_f(2) = B(0, 1)/B(0, 2) - 1 = 0.925926/0.849454 - 1 = 9.0025\%$. This immediately implies the yield volatilities do not affect these forward rates.

b) These rates were computed by formulas such as

$$r_e(2) = \frac{r_u + r_d}{2} \tag{47}$$

and

$$r_e(3) = \frac{1}{B(0,2)}\left(\frac{1}{2(1+r_d)}\frac{r_{dd}+r_{du}}{2} + \frac{1}{2(1+r_u)}\frac{r_{du}+r_{uu}}{2}\right). \tag{48}$$

c) From Table 4, we see that the difference between the two settlement styles is larger for the high volatility tree (#1) for the Year 2 and 3 forward rates. In addition, the difference is larger for the later years. In looking at the short-rate trees, we see that the short rate tree #1 has a lower dispersion in Year 4 (ranging from 7.55 percent to 15.81 percent) than it does in tree #2 (ranging from 7.28 percent to 16.28 percent). This causes the difference for the five-year rates to be more pronounced for tree #2.

## Question 25.16

a) The probability transition matrix looks as follows:

|       | [,1]      | [,2]      | [,3]       | [,4]      | [,5]      |
|-------|-----------|-----------|------------|-----------|-----------|
| [1,]  | 0.7616667 | 0.1766667 | 0.06166667 | 0.0000000 | 0.0000000 |
| [2,]  | 0.1029167 | 0.6441667 | 0.25291667 | 0.0000000 | 0.0000000 |
| [3,]  | 0.0000000 | 0.1666667 | 0.66666667 | 0.1666667 | 0.0000000 |
| [4,]  | 0.0000000 | 0.0000000 | 0.25291667 | 0.6441667 | 0.1029167 |
| [5,]  | 0.0000000 | 0.0000000 | 0.06166667 | 0.1766667 | 0.7616667 |

b) The price of a five-year 7.5 percent interest rate cap on a $1 million notional amount is equal to 0.0126424.

## Question 25.18

We can model a discrete version of equation 25.26:

$$r_i - r_{i-1} = a\left(b - r_{i-1} + \sigma\Phi\right)h + \sigma\sqrt{h}z_i$$

It is important not to forget the risk premium adjustment in the risk-neutral process when simulating.

The following shows you results for 50 steps and 20000 simulations. As you see, it comes quite close to the theoretical solution. You can obtain the theoretical solution by implementing equation 25.31 or by using the Excel spreadsheet that comes with the book.

We get for the following parameters r = 0.06, a = 0.2, b = 0.08, $\Phi$ = 0.05, and $\sigma$ = 0.02:

| Maturity | Theoretical Price | Simulation |
|----------|-------------------|------------|
| T = 1    | 0.939616          | 0.939710   |
| T = 2    | 0.879510          | 0.879473   |
| T = 3    | 0.820841          | 0.820593   |

## Question 25.20

We can model a discrete version of equation 25.26, with the CIR $\sqrt{r_{i-1}}$ term in the standard deviation:

$$r_i - r_{i-1} = a\left(b - r_{i-1} + \overline{\Phi r_{i-1}}\right)h + \sigma\sqrt{r_{i-1}}\sqrt{h}z_i$$

You may wonder where the adjustment term for the risk premium is coming from. Remember that the adjustment term in equation 25.26 is $\sigma(r)\Phi(r,t)$. In the Cox, Ingersoll, and Ross model, you can show that $\Phi(r,t) = \overline{\Phi}\frac{\sqrt{r}}{\sigma}$ (see equation 25.33), and we know that $\sigma(r) = \sigma\sqrt{r}$. Hence, $\sigma(r)\Phi(r,t) = \overline{\Phi}r$.

The numerical problem the question asks about is the following. Because we use a discretized version of the process in our simulations, $r$ can become negative, but we have a term $\sqrt{r_{i-1}}$ in the equation above. You can avoid numerical problems by replacing $\sqrt{r_{i-1}}$ with a small positive number whenever $r_{i-1}$ is negative.

The following shows you results for 50 steps and 20,000 simulations. As you see, it comes quite close to the theoretical solution. You can obtain the theoretical solution by implementing equation 25.34 or by using the Excel spreadsheet that comes with the book.

We get for the following parameters $r = 0.06$, $a = 0.2$, $b = 0.08$, $\Phi = 0$, and $\sigma = 0.02$:

| Maturity | theoretical price | simulation |
|----------|-------------------|------------|
| T = 1    | 0.940005          | 0.940049   |
| T = 2    | 0.880727          | 0.880753   |
| T = 3    | 0.822993          | 0.823057   |

Again, theoretical and simulated prices are quite close.

# Chapter 26

## Value at Risk

### Question 26.2

A 95 percent, VaR uses $Z_1 = -1.645$, and the 99 percent VaR uses $Z_2 = -2.326$. Given the horizon $h$ (in years), the value of 10 million will be $10e^{(\alpha - \sigma^2/2)h + \sigma\sqrt{h}Z_i}$ million. Table 1 shows these values as well as the loss (VaR).

### Table 1 (Problem 26.2)

**95%**

| Values | 1 day | 10 day | 20 day |
|---|---|---|---|
| A | 9,747,824 | 9,242,241 | 8,960,529 |
| B | 9,622,055 | 8,866,025 | 8,445,521 |
| Loss (VaR) | 1 day | 10 day | 20 day |
| A | 252,176 | 757,759 | 1,039,471 |
| B | 377,945 | 1,133,975 | 1,554,479 |

**99%**

| Values | 1 day | 10 day | 20 day |
|---|---|---|---|
| A | 9,644,067 | 8,934,714 | 8,541,801 |
| B | 9,468,836 | 8,427,213 | 7,860,500 |
| Loss (VaR) | | | |
| A | 355,933 | 1,065,286 | 1,458,199 |
| B | 531,164 | 1,572,787 | 2,139,500 |

### Question 26.4

The portfolio mean is $\alpha_p = 16.3$ percent and the standard deviation is $\sigma_p = 28.65$ percent. Letting $h$ be the holding period, there is a 95 percent (or 99 percent) chance the value of the portfolio will exceed

$$\$10\text{m} \times \left[ 1 + \alpha_p h + \sigma_p \sqrt{h} Z_i \right] \tag{4}$$

where $Z_1 = -1.645$ (95 percent) and $Z_2 = -2.326$ (99 percent). See Table 3 for the numerical answers.

## Table 3 (Problem 26.4)

| Values | 1 day | 10 day | 20 day |
|---|---|---|---|
| 95% | 9,757,785 | 9,264,584 | 8,986,124 |
| 99% | 9,655,581 | 8,941,387 | 8,529,054 |
| Loss (VaR) | 1 day | 10 day | 20 day |
| 95% | 242,215 | 735,416 | 1,013,876 |
| 99% | 344,419 | 1,058,613 | 1,470,946 |

## Question 26.6

The 100,000 105-strike, one-year put options have a premium of $1,026,694.90; hence, $W = 11,026,694$. The delta (per share) is $-0.3997$. Using equations (26.10) and (26.11), we obtain

$$R_p = \frac{0.15 \times 100}{W}\left(100000\left(1 - 0.3997\right)\right) = 0.081656 \tag{6}$$

and

$$\sigma_p = \frac{100^2 \times 0.3^2}{W^2}\left(100,000\left(1 - 0.3997\right)\right)^2 = 0.16331. \tag{7}$$

Table 5 shows the six VaR values using the normal approximation.

## Table 5 (Problem 26.6)

| | 95% | | | 99% | | |
|---|---|---|---|---|---|---|
| | 1 day | 10 day | 20 day | 1 day | 10 day | 20 day |
| Value | 10,874,121 | 10,561,083 | 10,382,670 | 10,809,886 | 10,357,951 | 10,095,399 |
| Loss (VaR) | 152,574 | 465,612 | 644,025 | 216,809 | 668,743 | 931,296 |

## Question 26.8

We first do the problem analytically; since we have written options, we receive the premiums, which is $1,571,210. It is virtually impossible for $S$ to fall enough in a week for there to be a loss ($Z \approx -5.64$). The 95 percent, 10-day VaR is, therefore, the loss when $Z = 1.645$; with this value, the option position will be $1,901,066, which is a loss of $329,856. Monte Carlo simulations should confirm this.

The delta of our position is $-100,000 (-0.22128 + 0.539417) = -31,814$. If we use the delta approximation, we could use a normal approximation with return

$$R_p = \frac{100,000}{1,571,210}0.15\left(100\right)\left(0.318135\right) = 30.372\% \tag{8}$$

and variance

$$\sigma_p^2 = \frac{100^2 (31{,}814)^2 \cdot 3^2}{1{,}571{,}210^2} = 36.899\% \, . \tag{9}$$

Using a normal approximation, the value of our portfolio would be

$$W_h = -1{,}571{,}210\left(1 + R_p \frac{10}{365} + \sigma_p \sqrt{\frac{10}{365}} Z\right). \tag{10}$$

Our profit is $W_h + 1{,}571{,}210$. If $Z = 1.645$, the profit will be negative; this amounts to a 95 percent, 10- day VaR of \$272,947, which is much less than the true VaR of \$329,856. This large error is due to the linear approximation of a highly nonlinear payoff. The payoff is similar to Figure 26.3. The negative delta of $-31{,}814$ underestimates the true loss due to a negative gamma.

## Question 26.10

As in problem 26.8, the loss occurs when the stock price rises, i.e., $Z = 1.645$. At this value the portfolio is worth $-1{,}901{,}066$. The conditional expected value of the portfolio should be approximately 2.025m leading to tail VaR that is approximately \$454,000. The simulation method is to sort the portfolio values and then take the average only of those simulations where the value is greater than 1.9m.

## Question 26.12

Since $8 = \frac{2}{3}7 + \frac{1}{3}10$, interpolation implies

$$y_8 = \frac{2}{3}(0.06) + \frac{1}{3}(0.065) = 0.06167 \tag{14}$$

$$\sigma_8 = \frac{2}{3}(0.10) + \frac{1}{3}(0.095) = 0.09833 \, . \tag{15}$$

The yield being 6.167 percent implies the bond position is worth $10e^{-0.06167(8)} = \$6.1059\text{m}$. Using these values, the 10-day, 95 percent VaR is

$$\$6.1059\text{m} \times \left(1 + 0.09833 \times 8 \times \sqrt{\frac{10}{365}} \times (-1.645)\right) - \$6.1059\text{m} = -\$1.31\text{m} \tag{16}$$

and a 10-day, 99 percent VaR of

$$\$6.1059\text{m} \times \left(1 + 0.09833 \times 8 \times \sqrt{\frac{10}{365}} \times (-2.326)\right) - \$6.1509\text{m} = -\$1.85\text{m}. \tag{17}$$

# Chapter 27

## Credit Risk

### Question 27.2

Using the formulas of the main text, we can calculate the following values for the yield, the probability of default, and the expected loss given default for all times to maturity:

| Years to Maturity | Yield | Probability of Default | Recovery | Expected Loss Given Default | Approx. |
|---|---|---|---|---|---|
| 1 | 0.215502281 | 0.5 | 74.65543 | 0.253445658 | 0.206723 |
| 2 | 0.169925969 | 0.5 | 67.07878 | 0.329212215 | 0.162303 |
| 3 | 0.150053883 | 0.5 | 62.09065 | 0.379093545 | 0.143182 |
| 4 | 0.138376782 | 0.5 | 58.35039 | 0.416496097 | 0.132062 |
| 5 | 0.130513667 | 0.5 | 55.36063 | 0.446393746 | 0.124639 |
| 10 | 0.111591282 | 0.5 | 45.8246 | 0.541753977 | 0.107088 |
| 20 | 0.099109428 | 0.5 | 36.47327 | 0.63526726 | 0.095882 |

Note that the probability of default is constant for the parameter values chosen. The last column of the above table shows the approximations. They work remarkably well.

### Question 27.4

a) We can calculate for a maturity value of $80:

| | | | | | | | |
|---|---|---|---|---|---|---|---|
| mat val | 80 | 80 | 80 | 80 | 80 | 80 | 80 |
| time to mat | 1 | 2 | 3 | 4 | 5 | 10 | 20 |
| bond price | 69.453 | 61.391 | 54.921 | 49.458 | 44.728 | 27.965 | 11.661 |
| yield | 0.141 | 0.132 | 0.125 | 0.120 | 0.116 | 0.105 | 0.096 |
| prob default | 0.288 | 0.347 | 0.374 | 0.390 | 0.401 | 0.430 | 0.450 |
| expected recovery | 63.489 | 57.044 | 52.754 | 49.526 | 46.940 | 38.688 | 30.614 |
| expected loss given default | 0.206 | 0.287 | 0.341 | 0.381 | 0.413 | 0.516 | 0.617 |

b)  For a maturity value of $120, we obtain:

| mat val | 120 | 120 | 120 | 120 | 120 | 120 | 120 |
|---|---|---|---|---|---|---|---|
| time to mat | 1 | 2 | 3 | 4 | 5 | 10 | 20 |
| bond price | 88.145 | 78.590 | 70.773 | 64.077 | 58.214 | 36.989 | 15.711 |
| yield | 0.309 | 0.212 | 0.176 | 0.157 | 0.145 | 0.118 | 0.102 |
| prob default | 0.676 | 0.626 | 0.604 | 0.590 | 0.581 | 0.557 | 0.541 |
| expected recovery | 83.723 | 75.660 | 70.264 | 66.186 | 62.912 | 52.390 | 41.971 |
| expected loss given default | 0.302 | 0.369 | 0.414 | 0.448 | 0.476 | 0.563 | 0.650 |

c)  For a maturity value of $80, the probability of default is increasing, and for a maturity value of $120, the probability of default is decreasing. If the maturity value is $80, we start out with a bond obligation that is well below our current asset threshold. Within a short time to maturity, it is more unlikely that the asset value decreases below the threshold of $80, but the likelihood increases with time to maturity. Conversely, with a maturity value of $120, we have a debt obligation that is considerably higher than our current asset value. The initial probability of default is very high. The longer we allow the asset price to develop, the more likely it is that it drifts upward and that the assets increase beyond the threshold of $120.

# Question 27.6

We can calculate the following values for the bond prices, yields, and expected losses for the model with and without jump risk:

|  | Without jump risk | With jump risk |
|---|---|---|
| mat val | 110 | 110 |
| time to mat | 5 | 5 |
| bond price | 55.278 | 47.098 |
| yield | 0.1376 | 0.1506 |

Incorporating jump risk makes the bond less valuable and thus increases the yield.

## Question 27.8

Using the different maturities, we obtain the following yields:

| Time to mat | 1 | 2 | 3 | 4 | 5 | 10 | 20 |
|---|---|---|---|---|---|---|---|
| Equity | 11.855 | 21.407 | 29.185 | 35.751 | 41.367 | 60.065 | 75.500 |
| Bond price | 88.145 | 78.593 | 70.815 | 64.249 | 58.633 | 39.935 | 24.500 |
| Yield | 0.309 | 0.212 | 0.176 | 0.156 | 0.143 | 0.110 | 0.079 |
| Terminal Prob default | 0.654 | 0.521 | 0.420 | 0.344 | 0.287 | 0.144 | 0.062 |
| intermediary Probability of default | 0.011 | 0.053 | 0.093 | 0.126 | 0.153 | 0.234 | 0.304 |
| Total probability of default | 0.665 | 0.574 | 0.513 | 0.470 | 0.440 | 0.378 | 0.366 |

We can see that the yields are continuously decreasing with maturity. The probabilities of default are going down, suggesting that the bond becomes progressively less risky.

## Question 27.10

The answer to these questions can be read directly from the transition matrix:

| Four-Year Matrix | | | |
|---|---|---|---|
| | F | FF | FFF |
| F | 0.72089 | 0.211302 | 0.067809 |
| FF | 0.401668 | 0.507982 | 0.090351 |
| FFF | 0.345313 | 0.470535 | 0.184153 |

An FF rating is retained with 50.8 percent probability; a rating change happens with 49.2 percent probability.

An FFF rating is retained with 18.4 percent probability; an FFF rated company changes its rating with 81.6 percent probability.

## Question 27.12

Following the procedure in the main textbook, we can write:

| Number of Defaults | Proba | Total Payoff | Bond Payoff Tranche1 | Tranche2 | Tranche3 |
|---|---|---|---|---|---|
| 0 | 0.9 | 300 | 160 | 50 | 90 |
| 1 | 0 | 240 | 160 | 50 | 30 |
| 2 | 0 | 180 | 160 | 20 | 0 |
| 3 | 0.1 | 120 | 120 | 0 | 0 |
| Price | | | 146.9153 | 42.3794 | 76.28293 |
| Yield | | | 0.085318 | 0.165361 | 0.165361 |
| Default probability | | | 0.1 | 0.1 | 0.1 |
| Average recovery rate | | | 0.75 | 0 | 0 |

## Question 27.14

Using the same methodology as before, but extending the number of bonds in the portfolio, we can calculate for 5, 10, 20, and 50 bond portfolios:

| | First-to-Default | Second-to-Default | Fifth-to-Default |
|---|---|---|---|
| Expected Payoff | 75.39228 | 95.11315 | 99.99402 |
| Price | 71.00178 | 89.57419 | 94.17082 |
| Yield | 0.342465 | 0.110103 | 0.06006 |

| | First-to-Default | Second-to-Default | 10th-to-Default |
|---|---|---|---|
| Expected Payoff | 60.33097 | 83.77231 | 100 |
| Price | 56.81757 | 78.89379 | 94.17645 |
| Yield | 0.565325 | 0.237068 | 0.06 |

| | First-to-Default | Second-to-Default | 20th-to-Default |
|---|---|---|---|
| Expected Payoff | 46.48988 | 62.85515 | 100 |
| Price | 43.78252 | 59.19475 | 94.17645 |
| Yield | 0.825936 | 0.524337 | 0.06 |

|                  | First-to-Default | Second-to-Default | 50th-to-Default |
| ---------------- | ---------------- | ----------------- | --------------- |
| Expected Payoff  | 40.29309         | 41.79444          | 100             |
| Price            | 37.9466          | 39.36052          | 94.17645        |
| Yield            | 0.96899          | 0.932407          | 0.06            |

You can see a dramatic increase in the yields of the first- and second-to-default bonds the more bonds are included in the portfolio. However, for the $N$th-to-default bond, there is little variation in the yield. Already with five included bonds, it is virtually risk free, i.e., the probability of all five uncorrelated bonds defaulting at the same time is almost zero.